D0762232

POSTWAR ECONOMIC GROWTH

POSTWAR ECONOMIC GROWTH

Four Lectures

By SIMON KUZNETS

THE BELKNAP PRESS OF
HARVARD UNIVERSITY PRESS

CAMBRIDGE, MASSACHUSETTS · 1964

FOREWORD

THESE LECTURES were delivered under the auspices of The John Randolph and Dora Haynes Foundation during the week of March 30, 1964. The first lecture was presented to the Economic Section of the Town Hall Forum of Los Angeles; the other three at the University of California, Riverside. I am grateful to the Haynes Foundation for the opportunity, and to the administration and faculty of the University of California, Riverside, for the hospitable arrangements provided.

Like my other papers dealing with economic growth, the present lectures draw heavily upon work in the field initiated under the auspices of the Committee on Economic Growth of the Social Science Research Council. Miss Lillian Epstein rendered valuable assistance in checking the tables and editing the text. I am also much indebted to Professor Alexander Gerschenkron of Harvard University and to Professor Moses Abramovitz of Stanford University for helpful comments which were utilized in the revision.

Simon Kuznets

CONTENTS

TABLES

POSTWAR ECONOMIC GROWTH

Lecture I

WORLD ECONOMIC STRUCTURE: DIVERSITY AND INTERDEPENDENCE

THE ECONOMIC structure and growth of the world can be studied best if we view mankind as organized into nation-states, each sovereign over its territory and people, each with a government responsible for overriding and major decisions, and each organizing a society that has common bonds sufficient to assure the effectiveness of many of these decisions. This use of the nation-state as the primary unit of study seems to me valid, despite extensive international relations, the United Nations, the Common Market, the Communist International, the Arab League, and other regional unions, on the one hand; and the *intra*-national frictions that erupt so frequently and so violently in newspaper headlines, on the other. With reference to economic structure and growth, in particular, the nation-state appears to be the locus of decisions that set the conditions under which economic activities are conducted. It may be fair to say that one main function of the modern sovereign state, with its assumed perpetual life and its dominant power within the society that it organizes, is to establish the conditions indispensable for the promotion of long-term economic growth—no matter how unsuccessful the attempt often is. It is hardly an accident that recent decades have witnessed the formation of many new nation-states, and drastic political changes in many others—all in the explicitly stated aspiration of the societies concerned to be masters of their economic and social destinies.

The number of such nation-states in the world varies: it depends upon the date and even more upon our decision to include or exclude such curious splinters as Andorra, Monaco, and so on, and the few territorial possessions that still exist. But if we omit all of these, large in number but accounting for a minute fraction of the world's population, considerably more than 100 nation-states remain and they display a wide diversity with respect to (a) size, (b) natural endowments, (c) economic performance, (d) economic structure, (e) political and social organization, and (f) many other economically relevant aspects of their historical heritage. Although it must be superficial, a brief discussion of this vast subject will provide a background against which the implications of diversity among nations combined with their interdependence, the main theme of this lecture, can be explored.

(a) The size of a nation can be gauged, to use simple criteria, by its population, by its area, or, for our purpose, by its economic output. If we begin with population, the contrast in 1958 (the year covered in Table 1) between, say, 1.2 million for Costa Rica and over 650 million for Mainland China is patent enough. In Table 1, total world population for 1958 is set at 2.9 billion, and 139 country units are distinguished— a smaller number than those in existence. Thus, of some 150 nation-states, just four—Mainland China, India, U.S.S.R., and the United States—account for 1.4 billion, or close to half of the world total.

Size measured by area, although a less important criterion than population, reveals similar contrasts. Total area, including inland water and uninhabited stretches of land, but excluding wholly uninhabited areas, measures about 22.4 million square kilometers for the U.S.S.R., between 9 and 10 million for Mainland China, for the United States, and for Canada, just 244 thousand for the United Kingdom, about 43 thousand for Denmark, and only about 10 thousand for Lebanon. The four largest countries (U.S.S.R., Mainland China, United States, and Canada) account for 51.4 million, or close to four-tenths of the total area of the world, 135.2 million square kilometers. And the area of any one of scores of countries is well below 10,000 square kilometers.[1]

The comparison of economic output, whether it is measured by gross domestic product at factor cost (used in Tables 1 and 2 at the end of this lecture) or some other aggregate derived from national accounts, is subject to many qualifications, touched upon briefly below. According to Table 1, which exaggerates the differences in terms of purchasing power, the distribution of countries by gross domestic product is even more skewed than those by population and area. The United States alone accounts for some 35 percent of the world total— questionable as such a total may be. And the total for the United States and the U.S.S.R. is close to one-half of the world's economic output. At the other end of the range are many countries with gross domestic product well below a billion dollars.

One may wonder whether, with such striking differences, nation-states really belong to one species; and the answer to this question depends upon whether the aspects of social life to be studied are crucially dependent on size. Without doubt, this combination of a few giant nations with many much smaller units is a characteristic of world structure that is relevant to our main theme.

(b) Since nations are spread out across the face of the

---

[1] The data in this paragraph are from United Nations, *Demographic Yearbook, 1961* (New York, 1961), Tables 1 and 2, pp. 101-20.

globe, and since their areas differ so much, their natural endowments—climate, soil, minerals, waterways, coast lines, and the like—all of which affect economic opportunities, also differ widely. To be sure, the economic significance of any one set of natural conditions varies with changes in material and social technology; and the term "endowment" suggests this, for what was useless yesterday may be an endowment today. But this still means that, for a given available complex of technology, natural conditions differ in economic significance; and may well have contributed greatly to the differences in the size of nations (and other characteristics) as they emerged from the historical past. One wonders, for example, whether the very large societies in China and India became established long before others because intensive, high-yield (per acre) agriculture was possible under their natural conditions, even though the formation and survival of unified organized states in these two areas and not in others similarly endowed must be explained by other factors.

Two aspects of diversity in natural endowments may be usefully distinguished. The first is a matter of sheer size, in the sense that differences in area usually mean differences in the magnitude of the natural resource base—more land, more minerals, more water, and so on, in the larger area unit; and the configuration of the area and the nature of its endowments may explain the formation in the past of national units of differing size. The second is a matter of endowment *relative* to the population; and here the potentialities of modern technology and the demands of the more developed countries are important. From the standpoint of the latter, the kind and relative supplies of natural resources in which various nations have comparative advantage differ widely, since the natural resources demanded by modern technology are scarce, and therefore are not likely to be evenly distributed across the face of the globe—at least not in terms of economic accessibility and cost. Thus the uneven distribution of natural resources, over and above their size, is another aspect of diversity that has implications for our main theme—for it sets the conditions for one type of interdependence that will be discussed below.

(c) A common over-all measure of a country's economic performance is total output per capita—on the realistic assumption that it is also a relative index of per worker productivity, since the variation in the ratio of labor force to total population is fairly limited. We face a problem, of course, in reducing to comparable units the outputs of countries that differ widely in the composition of the goods baskets and even in the quality of presumably similar goods.

The gross domestic product figures in Tables 1 and 2 have been converted to comparable units by means of money exchange rates—a device that uses easily available data but tends to exaggerate the differences in purchasing power among developed and underdeveloped countries. Indeed, the range is so wide that one may question the significance of the measures—even disregarding the differing magnitudes of purely statistical error. Thus, in 1958, the per capita gross domestic product of the United States was set at $2,324 and that of India at $67, a ratio of some 35 to 1. And, since household consumption accounts for a high proportion of gross product, per capita household expenditures for the two must have been in a ratio of close to 30 to 1.

Yet, granted the statistical errors and the index-number problems, there has perhaps been too much rejection recently of such quantitative comparisons. One should beware of this easy dismissal of these valuable, although crude, indications of differences in the economic performance of nations. While the specific magnitudes and ratios should not be accepted at face value, and minor disparities should be disregarded, three conclusions from such estimates seem valid.

First, a disparity in per capita product estimates of the order of more than 2 to 1, and even narrower for developed countries with similar structure and for which the estimates are of high quality, is a valid indication that the aggregate production of commodities and services per capita in the one country is significantly lower than in the other. Second, truly wide divergences—like that between the United States and India, or even of 10 to 1—are more telling, for they indicate that the structures and patterns of economic and social life must be quite different in the two countries. Even if we allow for the usual errors of estimation, such wide differences in per capita output would be impossible if the mode of life in the two societies were the same—with respect to family structure, degree of urbanization, education of the population, and the whole set of social institutions and prevailing beliefs that affect the masses of the population (not the small specialized elites). Third, if, as Table 2 suggests, over one-half of the world's population live in countries whose average per capita product (at factor cost) is less than $100, and six-tenths live in countries with per capita product below $200 per year, whereas only a seventh live in countries with per capita product of over $700, obviously most of mankind have not yet tapped at all adequately the potential of economic growth provided by modern technology—even though the per capita product of most of the less economically developed six-tenths of mankind is today probably higher than it was in the nineteenth and early twentieth centuries.

(d) Great disparities in per capita income are associated with wide differences in economic structure, which partly explain and partly corroborate the former by indicating how populations adjust to low (or high) per capita productivity. Thus low per capita product is associated with low productivity in most sectors, but particularly in agriculture; with a large proportion of the labor force attached to agriculture and required to feed the population;[2] with a dominance of small individual enterprises, not only in farming and handicrafts, but also in transport, finance, and other services; with a low degree of urbanization; with a greater persistence of the extended family system; and with a dependence upon foreign sources for the products of advanced technology that the country may need or afford. It is only in a few commodities, in demand by the more developed areas, that a low-income country may have a comparative advantage and thus can pay for the products and tools of modern technology. But, by definition, these opportunities of comparative advantage are not sufficient to raise over-all per capita product above low levels.

These antecedents of low per capita product in industrial structure and the pattern of organization of the productive system naturally affect the structure of consumption and pattern of life in general. Food is a dominant proportion of total consumer expenditures; but even at that, calorie consumption is relatively low, and a high proportion of the latter is in the form of starchy staples, not protective proteins and the like. With a predominantly rural population the costly necessities of urban life are minimal. Savings and capital formation proportions are low. Education is enjoyed by a limited fraction of the school-age population, and illiteracy is high. Thus the population "adjusts," if that is the proper term, to low per capita product by allocating most of its income to consumption, and within consumption, by restricting resource-input into goods that are not prime life

---

[2] For present purposes, this statement should be interpreted to mean that the large proportion of the labor force is attached to agriculture either because its full employment is required, under conditions of low productivity, to supply the population; or, partly because it has no opportunities elsewhere and is thus far from fully employed on land.

necessities; but the population still exhibits some vital consequences of a deficient standard of living.

All these familiar observations, if expressed in opposites, apply to the economic structure of high-income countries. The latter usually have high productivity in most sectors, but particularly in agriculture; a low proportion of the labor force attached to agriculture; a dominance of large-scale impersonally organized enterprises; a high degree of urbanization; a small nuclear family as the prevailing pattern of family structure; a low proportion of foods and high proportions of durable consumer goods and health, educational, and recreational services in household consumption; relatively high savings and capital formation proportions; and relatively full access within the country (unless it is quite small) to products of modern technology. The high-income countries may find themselves at a comparative disadvantage in regard to some agricultural and mineral goods; but dependence for these on supplies from abroad—usually from the less developed countries—is not large enough to jeopardize the high level of domestic productivity.

The contrasts among nations with respect to these aspects of economic structure, associated with wide disparities in per capita product, are indicated by a variety of evidence from comparative economic studies. Table 3 illustrates some of these diversities, and could be extended by varying the number and identity of the countries covered but at a cost of additional labor that did not seem warranted. Only two aspects of the widely known differences in economic structure among nations in the world today need be briefly indicated.

First, there are always exceptions to the typical economic structure of a country: islands of modernity in the sea of traditional life in the less developed countries, and areas of backwardness in those that are most developed. This does not mean, of course, that the major contrasts between the two are not valid: for the per worker productivity of even the more backward regions or sectors of a developed country may be much higher than that of most sectors in a less developed country. But it does mean that there are disparities within a country in productivity and organization among its sectors, regions, and groups that set up strains and stresses, that represent opportunities or dangers. The opportunities are offered by the more advanced sectors, regions, and so on, from which the growth-producing stimuli may spread to other parts of the economy; and the dangers are associated with the backward areas or sectors, which, by resisting change and claiming extra benefits, may constitute a drag upon the more advanced parts of an economy. Neither the movement toward a higher economic level, nor economic stagnation, is automatic.

Second, high-income countries have, in general, experienced substantial growth from the time in the past when they entered the period of modern economic growth (different for different countries) to the present; whereas the low-income countries are usually at that level because their income has either stagnated over long periods or risen quite slowly. This association between per capita income levels today and rates of growth in per capita income in the recent but long-term past, implies also an association between per capita income levels today and the rapidity of past changes in economic structure, what might be called internal economic change and mobility. It follows that those low-income countries that have not undergone revolutionary changes recently possess an economic structure built-in over a long period of no or little change, internal shift, or mobility; whereas the economic structure of the high-income countries has over a long period been experiencing marked changes—in the distribution among industries, in the pattern of organization of the economic unit or firm, in the structure of consumption—that should have generated mechanisms of relatively easy economic mobility within the country.

(e) The relevance of the distinction in Table 1 between Communist and non-Communist countries to a discussion of the economic structure of the world today need hardly be elaborated. Over a third of world population now lives in countries with Communist governments; and the total output of these countries is somewhat short of a quarter of the world total.[3] Of course, within the Communist bloc there is a marked contrast between China and the major Communist satellites in Asia (North Korea, North Vietnam), on the one hand, and the U.S.S.R. and Eastern European Communist countries, on the other—not only in per capita product but also in the militancy of the respective party dictatorships.

The two major groups within the non-Communist countries in Table 1 are distinguished by economic level and structure; and the contrast between the developed and the less developed non-Communist countries is quite clear. But in the present connection we are concerned with diversity in *political* structure: it is the possible differences in political and related aspects of social organization within the large group of non-Communist countries that are of interest.

Identification of the countries in the developed and less developed groups among non-Communist countries suggests some differences in recent political experience. The developed group is dominated by countries that have had a stable govern-

---

[3] This count may be viewed as incomplete, since Cuba and Ghana are here included among less developed non-Communist countries. Several others among the latter are also governed dictatorially by a single party, hostile to the West. They must be taken into consideration in any analysis of the grouping of nations by political orientation; but I have no firm basis for such a selective grouping.

ment, based upon a more or less similar and working democratic system, for a number of decades—the United Kingdom, the Scandinavian countries, Belgium, the Netherlands, and Switzerland in Europe; and the United States, Canada, Australia, and New Zealand overseas. These countries account for at least six-tenths of the 550 million people covered under non-Communist developed countries in Table 1.

Of the remaining countries in that group, a number— Germany, Italy, Japan, France—went through violent changes in political regime before and during the war. These varied in magnitude from country to country. Yet, each followed an antecedent long period of political stability and continuity that provided the foundation for a viable and continuous regime immediately, or with some delay, after World War II.

By contrast, the political regimes of many of the countries in the less developed non-Communist group, have been established quite recently, and in many cases after decades of colonial status. Among these, India, Pakistan, and Indonesia alone account for about eight-tenths of the total of 762 million in line 15 of Table 1; and the addition of Burma, Ceylon, Malaya, the Philippines, and Taiwan would raise the fraction still higher. Most of the countries in the Middle East and Africa, except Turkey and Iran and the Union of South Africa and Ethiopia, are also in this category. Of the 1.1 billion people in the less developed non-Communist group in Asia and Africa, perhaps eight-tenths or more are living in newly established nation-states, with a long and recent colonial history.

The political structure of Latin America, and of less developed Europe, raises additional questions. Both areas have been organized in formally independent political units for a long time—certainly far longer than most non-Communist countries in Asia and Africa and, for that matter, longer than the Communist countries. Political stability, however, has not been truly characteristic of Latin America; and Spain, the most populous unit of less developed Europe, is under a dictatorship, following a bitter civil war. I cannot say with any assurance that the lack of a stable, responsive, and continuous political organization in much of Latin America is the result of a distinctive internal structure of the economy and society, characterized by wide social and economic inequalities, and in many countries by a cleavage between the large traditional Indian components and the small groups of descendants, pure or mixed, of the immigrants, old or recent, from the southern European countries. It may fairly be said, however, that despite a long period of political independence, most Latin American countries do not enjoy political stability and continuity.

If one adds to the observations just made the obvious comment that the origin of the Communist bloc was recent and violent, and that countries within it have witnessed a continuous conflict between the policies and plans of the ruling minorities and the desires of the masses of the population, it is difficult to escape the conclusion that only a small fraction of world population resides in the countries that have had, for any substantial length of time, continuous stable governments responsive in democratic fashion to the diverse and changing interests of their inhabitants. By far the greater proportion of world population resides in countries where the political structure has either recently shifted in a revolutionary fashion to a new and strenuous order dominated by a dictatorial minority party; or has only recently reached political independence, after a long colonial history, and is still subject to perturbations and uncertainties; or, despite a long period of formal political independence, is characterized by an internal structure that makes political stability difficult to achieve. Obviously, these varieties of political organization and experience condition much of the economic structure and growth in recent decades.

(f) The brief comments above touched upon diversity among nations in size, natural endowments, economic performance as reflected in per capita product, economic structure, and political organization. This list far from exhausts the economically relevant aspects of diversity; for nations of roughly the same size, economic structure, and even broad lines of political organization, display differences in social institutions, conceptions of their roles in the world, and dominant notions concerning relations of man to man and man to nature, that produce different patterns of social and economic behavior—within each nation and in its relation to others. But the limitations of space and knowledge prevent me from dealing with diversity among nations in this complex of social institutions and beliefs. All one can say is that, regardless of the relations between this complex and the economic and political organization, the former has a life of its own and is a product of long history—of those long stretches of historical past when the common links that bind the members of a nation and provide it with the bases of common action were forged. Some components of the social institutions and beliefs that emerged in response to economic and social problems of the day may persist beyond their usefulness, and thus may, while providing elements of stability, constitute obstacles to growth-promoting change. Other components may be introduced in the process of borrowing, voluntary or imposed, from the outside, and thus may act as stimuli toward change in the economic and social framework inherited from the past.

Relations exist among nations, however, that make the diversity among them not merely a matter of scholarly interest and analysis, but a condition that affects the immediate practical problems of any one country. It is, of course, the interdependence of nations that makes their diversity so much more important than it would be if they were merely to coexist in the world, each in isolation and each completely uninterested in and indifferent to the others. We turn now to a brief review of these relations.

2

Interdependence among nations is a function of accessibility and interest. By accessibility we mean the technological ease with which transportation and communication facilities permit flows, either material or spiritual, among nations, which, by definition, are separated in space from each other. By interest we mean the realization by some or most members of a given nation that an active contact with the rest of the world promises a positive contribution to the goals of that nation. The concept of interest embraces a variety of concerns, with a resulting variety of actual flows between nations, and it may be discussed briefly.

In connection with economic structure, the most familiar form of interest among nations lies in the possibilities of exchange arising out of complementarities and the international division of labor. Since different nations have comparative advantage with respect to different commodities and services, it is a matter of enormous gain to all concerned to exchange goods rather than try to produce all of them (or their substitutes). And in the case of small nations particularly, the proportions of foreign trade to total domestic output are high—whether these nations are less developed, with exports concentrated primarily in agricultural and mineral raw materials; or developed, with a more varied and industrialized composition of exports. Since there are often several suppliers (or buyers) of a given good, or of goods substitutable for each other, there is not only international exchange but also competition. The resulting international flows of commodities and services, and of capital funds and investments are familiar and need only be recalled here. In addition, the voluntary movement of people across boundaries, in response to differential opportunities among nations under peaceful conditions, brings men to the opportunities instead of moving the products.

But there are two other forms of interest, besides that resulting in international economic competition and exchange, or the economically responsive movements of migrants. One of these is related to goods or resources that, unlike goods subject to market exchange or competition and resources of materials and labor involved in economic production, can be used *without* diminishing the supply—so that use by one need not restrict use by others. A conspicuous example is the stock of scientific and technological knowledge, which is the common possession of mankind and even if used by one nation, is still available to others (except, in a limited fashion, in the absorption of scarce human talent or material capital). Thus, technological and social innovations based upon the stock of useful knowledge are of potential service to all—in the sense that they serve the needs of all mankind, and are usually, at least in modern times, so embodied as to be accessible well beyond the boundaries of the nations within which they originate. The existence of such a stock of knowledge available to all creates a common interest and thus another level of interdependence among nations, in that the increase in the productive capacity of any given nation depends, often in large part, upon innovations and technological and social progress in others.

The third form of interest is evident when we allow for the possibility that a given nation, or group or nations, attempts a pre-emptive action to limit or reduce the economic resources and capacities of others by acts or threats of aggression based on power. In this case there is no *quid pro quo* in peaceful exchange, and no question of a common stock of resources available to all nations; but rather the employment of a given nation's power and presumptive superiority to reduce, if not the actual economic performance of others, their potential use of that capacity along lines that they prefer. Such policies of pressure and aggression, not uncommon in the recent past and in different and changing forms today, create lines of forcible interdependence—in that no nation can remain indifferent to these policies, whether or not they are at the moment aimed directly at it.

This rather sketchy and general formulation of the three levels of interdependence among nations is, perhaps, sufficient to suggest why and how the combination of such interdependence with the aspects of diversity indicated above is productive of many stresses and strains, makes for continuous turmoil in the world, and is pregnant with great dangers and also great opportunities.

Consider, for example, the combination of the various lines of interdependence with the contrast today between developed and underdeveloped non-Communist nations. At the level of international economic exchange, the trade of countries with low per capita income is primarily with the developed countries; and the very inequality in per capita income and the dependence of the underdeveloped nations upon export of agricultural and mineral raw materials, with many of them subject to uncertain production controls, may cause the economically weaker partners to view, perhaps unwarrantedly, differences in economic power as sources of exploitation rather than of fair exchange. And this is not to deny the huge economic gains from such trade, in obtaining at far lower costs than domestic production would entail the products of advanced technology embodying knowledge and expertise. When the underdeveloped nation is small and exports are oriented toward one large developed country, the situation is aggravated by such dependence and by the fact that the trade forms a high proportion of the national product of the small, less developed country, and a minute fraction of the national product of the large developed partner. When the less developed country is large, the major source of strain is the difficulty of generating enough exports to permit imports of producers' goods, domestically unavailable, and yet needed for an acceptable rate of growth.

The implication of the contrast between developed and underdeveloped nations is different when we consider ties created by a common stock of useful knowledge. Here also the underdeveloped nations are dependent on the stock of knowledge which in modern times has been created primarily in the developed countries, and may therefore be somewhat biased in that it has not been directed sufficiently toward the technical and social problems specific to less developed countries. It is almost impossible for the latter to acquire the highly trained skills and capacities associated with the use of modern knowledge without the help of the more developed nations. Yet the development of these modern trained groups and their proper integration, despite some alienation produced by such training, within the framework of the less developed countries is productive of stresses due either to the maladjustment of the educated unemployed or to the monopolistic position of these small elites that hinders the democratic organization of society. At the other end, the developed countries also suffer, because the large proportion of uneducated mankind that lives under poor economic and social conditions can make only a slight creative contribution to the stock of useful knowledge. Given the same universal distribution of native abilities, the blockage and waste of talent within the less developed countries represent a great loss to all mankind, the developed countries included.

Consider next the relations between diversity in size and the interdependence among nations. Whether developed or underdeveloped, a small nation suffers from the disadvantages of a limited internal market and division of labor, and must rely heavily on foreign trade—which, in the case of close proximity to a much larger developed nation, often places it in a satellitic position to the latter. Under these conditions, the economic advantage, although great, may give rise to strains produced by the fear of losing independence and identity. But, more important, under conditions of hostility and aggression, in the past and even more today, the dependence of small nations on their large allies for protection impedes the pursuit of an independent policy, even in the economic field; and for the large nation in a position of leadership, which may have been thrust upon it, this means a further responsibility in addition to the internal problems that arise in the course of economic and social change. It is in this connection that the diversity in size stressed above—viz., the coexistence of a few large nations with many small nations—is most directly relevant. It creates the basis for the formation of blocs; and the interlocking of national and bloc policies and interest raises problems that are productive of further international strain.

We come finally to diversity of political organization, which is most obvious in its bearing upon interdependence among nations. The emergence of the Communist bloc, devoted, with varying degrees of intensity, to the proposition that a large group of nations—the "capitalist" countries—are evil because of their economic and social organization, and that vituperative hostility is the proper attitude, is clearly a disruptive factor creating major difficulties.[4] It affects the mechanism of international economic exchange and competition, creating difficult trading problems and enforcing a "politicization" of foreign trade and other flows across boundaries that causes tremendous economic waste. It creates a climate of hostility and instability conducive to the allocation of huge resources to the preservation of national and world security. It thereby creates an interdependence of nations that distorts the domestic and foreign policy, economic and other, of the developed non-Communist countries, and represents, from their standpoint and for that matter from the standpoint of all mankind, enormous waste of economic capacity. The policy of hostility overt in the Communist-bloc attitudes toward the developed world beyond the Iron Curtain may be an effective device for strengthening the morale of their population and infusing it, by design, with a sense of unity in order to facilitate acceptance of the harsh realities of dictatorially forced capital accumulation; but the effects, in the present connection, of this particular link between diversity and interdependence remain real and disturbing.

The divisive effect of the combination of certain costly lines of interdependence with the political diversity among nations, represented by the Communist-Capitalist dichotomy, is further aggravated not only by the emergence of many newly established states among the underdeveloped countries in Asia and Africa, but also by the failure of many older states in Latin America to attain political stability and continuity.

---

[4] These statements can easily be documented from official sources. Perhaps they should not be accepted at face value, in view of the perversion of language in its relation to the true content of underlying official Communist pronouncements. Nevertheless, it seems more valid to accept them, with some discount, than to deny their relevance completely.

The legacy of colonialism in the former facilitates attempts to attain unity by fostering hostility toward the developed non-Communist countries; and, not accidentally, a similar strain is now developing within the Communist bloc, in the relations between Mainland China and the U.S.S.R. Because their political organization is weak, many of the less developed nations are tempted to make excuses by blaming the devil of the past—a form of cultural lag, a failure to recognize the bearing of recent changes upon major policy questions, that is perhaps a natural result of the speed with which economic and social changes have been taking place throughout the world. But it must be remembered that both the political weakness of much of the underdeveloped world in Asia and Africa and its hostile attitudes toward the Western developed countries are the result of a long colonial history. They are a survival of the consequences of economic and political diversity among nations in the nineteenth and early twentieth centuries; and of the elements of aggression in the policies of the older developed nations toward those that lagged behind in the spread of modern economic growth.

3

The preceding comments are, perhaps, sufficient to suggest that the diversity among nations with respect to size, economic level and structure, and political organization, combined with interdependence stemming from economic exchange and competition, universal possession of a stock of knowledge and other creative attainments useful to all mankind, and divisive attitudes and policies of hostility and aggression, are productive of many stresses and problems, accompanying the substantial economic advance that has undoubtedly been attained in recent decades. We conclude by brief observations on: (a) the recent trends in diversity and interdependence; and (b) the relations between these aspects of world structure and the basic forces underlying modern economic growth.

(a) If to give us some perspective we shift our view of the world economic structure from today to a past period, say to the last half century but with emphasis on recent decades, the picture suggests that the range of several aspects of diversity among nations has widened, while the ties of interdependence have become stronger. And, as a result, the problems and strains that the combination of diversity and interdependence generates may have been intensified.

While we cannot document these observations here, and they must therefore remain tentative conjectures, some supporting illustrations are at hand. Thus, the contrast in per capita income between developed and underdeveloped countries must have widened appreciably over the last half century— at least between the group of non-Communist countries classified as developed in Table 1, and all less developed countries in Asia and Africa, including the Communist countries (the latter comprising something like two-thirds of world population today). Half a century ago the per capita income of the developed group was already much above that of the underdeveloped areas in Asia and Africa (that is, all except Japan); since that time per capita product grew at rates well over 10 percent and often over 20 percent per decade in the developed group while it grew much more slowly in the underdeveloped areas. Indeed, the contrast must widen by definition for any dichotomy in which we compare currently developed countries with currently underdeveloped areas—since any sustained participation in modern economic growth over a substantial period (say half a century) should shift a country from the underdeveloped to the developed group. A classification based on *present* levels and economic structure limits the underdeveloped group to countries that, by definition, grew more slowly than the units in the developed group; and widening of contrast in per capita income (over the long period as a whole) automatically follows. But even if we start with a dichotomy based on levels and structure at the *beginning*, not at the end, of a fairly long period such as half a century the contrast may still widen, *if* entry into modern economic growth, sustained industrialization, affects only a limited proportion of the initially underdeveloped group of countries (or, rather, population). And this is what happened: if we consider Japan and the U.S.S.R. as the two countries that shifted over that period from the underdeveloped to the developed group (admitting the U.S.S.R. into the latter category to strengthen the case) the population accounted for by this shift is only 0.3 billion out of a total of close to 2 billion in the underdeveloped parts of the world (outside of Latin America and Eastern Europe).

The trend (over the past half century) in diversity among nations by size is somewhat less certain, if we deal with nation-states, largely because of the major change from colonial status and dependency to political independence. A classification of the earlier colonial empires as single political units would reveal a decline in the number of huge political entities that would have been represented by the British, French, Japanese, and even the Dutch empires. But this trend would not have affected significantly the size of such giant nations as the United States, the U.S.S.R., and Mainland China; and, on the other hand, would show large additions to the number of small formally independent nation-states. In the skewed distribution of nation-states by size, the group at the small-size end of the range (as reflected in all three criteria used in the discussion above) was thus much increased; and the magnitude of diversity, measured, say, by the area in a Lorenz curve under the diagonal representing equal size, must have risen sharply. This was particularly true of the most recent decade, when political independence was attained by so many small units in Africa.

This recent growth in number of nation-states and the emergence of the Communist bloc within the last half century suggest that diversity in political organization has widened, in comparison with the time before World War I, and increasingly so in recent decades. True, in the past there were differences in political organization not observed today—for example, among absolute monarchies, constitutional monarchies, republics, and the like. Yet, at the danger of being dogmatic, one may argue that in their bearing upon economic structure and growth, the differences in political organization that have developed recently, those discussed in connection with Table 1, represent a widening of diversity among nation-states.

In particular, we should note the increase in the number of large countries that managed to tap the potential of modern economic growth. If we consider the United Kingdom, France, Germany, and the United States as the large developed countries early in the period, the emergence of Japan and the U.S.S.R. as developed countries meant a substantial *proportional* increase. And in view of the different historical background of these newcomers, the likelihood of strains in their relations with each other was all the greater.

In recent decades the widening diversity among independent nation-states in size, per capita economic product, economic structure, and political organization has been accompanied by significant strengthening or intensification of interdependence among nations. First, and most obvious, continuing innovations in transportation and communication have increased accessibility, and thus permitted far closer interdependence than would have been possible otherwise.

Second, if we set aside the difficult question whether international trade and related flows have kept pace with the growth of total world output, and *allow* for the restrictive effects of the autarkical Communist bloc, the very widening of diversity in per capita product, combined with the intensified drive toward economic adequacy and growth, increased the dependence of at least the underdeveloped countries upon the developed. Third, the strains of hostility and aggression introduced by the newly emergent lines of political organization have also made for greater interdependence among nations. Clearly under conditions of a cold war the ties among the participants, either on one side or among those on both, are much closer than under conditions of relative isolation and indifference. The closer interdependence between, say, the United States and the U.S.S.R. than that between this country and some distant developed non-Communist nation (like Australia), or than that between the United States and Czarist Russia before World War I, is a phenomenon too obvious to need stressing, even though the dependence is one of mutual watchfulness and sensitivity to security.

It would seem, then, that the trends toward widening diversity and more intensive interdependence may have induced the greater stresses and perturbations that characterize life today. We may now ask whether these trends have been associated with the forces and drives that underlie much of the economic growth in modern times.

(b) Before answering this question we must recognize the magnitude and source of modern economic growth—the topic of the second lecture in this series. But, forestalling this later discussion, we mention here that the major source of modern economic growth, with its high rates of aggregate increase and rapid structural shifts, lies in the vast increase in the stock of useful knowledge. Much of this knowledge is based on science and connected with widespread changes in the attitude of human beings to material welfare and in their capacity to exploit effectively the world around them to useful ends. Yet, the potential of ever-increasing economic achievement, permitted by the growth of science and technology, requires, if it is to be exploited, many social adjustments—rearrangements of the old established pre-modern social and political institutions—to generate the necessary capital, to permit adequate investment in the education and training of human beings, to facilitate the movement of individuals to the places of greatest economic opportunity, and to provide sufficient motivation and return so that growth becomes self-sustaining rather than self-limiting, because of bottlenecks resulting from monopolization of opportunities or resistance of obsolescent industries, occupations, and so on, to the necessary transition.

It is in this connection that the nation-state, as indicated in the opening paragraphs of this lecture, plays a major part by introducing and facilitating the essential adjustments in the social and economic institutions inherited from the past; and does so by means of its dominant power grounded in a social consensus that tolerates within the society the decline of some groups and the advance of others. Thus, the spread of the nation-state and its growing role in setting the conditions for economic growth may be viewed as a function partly of the greater potential of economic growth provided by the ever-growing complex of modern material and social technology; partly of the uneven spread in the utilization of this potential among nations which, while widening current diversities in economic level and structure, makes for an ever-increasing strain of backwardness. In a sense, the intensification of nationalism, with the resulting pressure to set up divisive self-centered nation-state units, is the price paid for the potential ability to channel the energies of societies so organized to the task of exploiting the promise of modern economic growth—exploiting it on the basis of a consensus stemming from some common bonds that sustain the society despite the disruptiveness of modern economic change. Modern economic growth is revolutionary in the rapidity of its structural shifts, the changes in relative position among various groups in society; and the modern nation-state is the mechanism usually employed to channel and contain such a revolution. I am not arguing that this is the only mechanism, or that all its current manifestations are indispensable to the task; but in the light of modern developments, the basic relevance of the nation-state to the task of economic growth seems patent.

From these observations it follows that the increasing diversity among nations with respect to size and political organization may well be a result of the extension of modern economic growth to many areas, and of the rapid growth of the potential power provided by modern technology—employable internally or externally. All of this makes adjustment to the increasing gap in economic, and hence political, power more and more difficult. Of particular importance may be an aspect only briefly noted above—the increase in the number of *large* nations that have managed to secure the power bestowed by modern economic growth, nations that almost inevitably are affected by different historical backgrounds and heritage. This increasing diversity among large and relatively developed nations themselves, in addition to diversity in size, is a potent source of increasing international strains and tension. And it is in this connection that the spread of modern economic growth and the striking rise in the potential of modern technology are productive of major dangers in the world structure of today; and, if these dangers can be avoided or damped, of great opportunities.

		GDP (billions) (1)	Population (millions) (2)	Per Capita GDP($) (3)	% of World Total GDP (4)	% of World Total Population (5)	Per Capita GDP (relative) (6)
		I. NON-COMMUNIST DEVELOPED COUNTRIES					
1.	United States and Canada	436.7	192.0	2,274	37.7	6.7	567
	a. United States	(406.5)	(174.9)	(2,324)	35.1	6.1	580
2.	Northern and Western Europe	145.9	139.6	1,045	12.6	4.8	261
3.	Other Europe	85.6	115.5	742	7.4	4.0	185
4.	Australia and New Zealand	14.9	12.1	1,227	1.3	0.4	306
5.	Japan	36.6	91.6	400	3.2	3.2	100
6.	Total, lines 1-5	719.7	550.8	1,307	62.2	19.1	326
		II. COMMUNIST COUNTRIES					
7.	U.S.S.R.	144.8	206.8	700	12.5	7.2	175
8.	Eastern Europe	68.9	114.8	600	6.0	4.0	150
9.	China	46.6	657.0	71	4.0	22.8	18
0.	Other Asia	1.8	24.7	71	0.2	0.9	18
1.	Total, lines 7-10	262.1	1,003.3	261	22.7	34.8	65
		III. NON-COMMUNIST LESS DEVELOPED COUNTRIES					
2.	Europe	14.4	47.7	301	1.2	1.7	75
3.	Latin America	58.9	199.7	295	5.1	6.9	74
4.	Middle East	17.7	100.7	176	1.5	3.5	44
5.	Asia[a]	57.7	762.6	76	5.0	26.4	19
	a. India	(27.6)	(411.9)	(67)	(2.4)	(14.3)	(17)
6.	Africa[b]	26.5	218.6	121	2.3	7.6	30
7.	Total, lines 12-16	175.2	1,329.2	132	15.1	46.1	33
8.	World total	1,157.0	2,883.3	401	100.0	100.0	100

Excludes Middle East and Japan; includes less developed Oceania.
Excludes Egypt.

NOTES

Non-Communist countries: Gross domestic product, total and per capita, was taken from United Nations, *Yearbook of National Accounts Statistics, 1962* (New York, 1963), Table 3, pp. 314ff. The only change made was in the per capita and total product estimates for Japan, because we felt that the 1958 per capita figure, $285 compared with $464 for 1961 (see *ibid.*, p. 316), underestimated performance in Japan; and we set it roughly at $400.

The population totals were derived by dividing total GDP by per capita product.
The following note from the source (p. 318) is relevant: "In converting GDP expressed in national currency units into U. S. dollars, the prevailing exchange rate was employed with a minimum of adjustment. For countries with a single fixed exchange rate system, the conversion rate chosen was normally the par value of the currency. For countries with a single fluctuating rate, the conversion rate was normally the annual average of import and export rates as reported by the IMF. For countries with multiple exchange rates, the conversion rate was normally an average of the

implicit rates obtained by comparing the values of exports and imports in dollars and in national currency units as reported by the IMF. . . . The estimates . . . should be considered as indicators of the total and per capita production of goods and services of the countries represented and not as measures of the standard of living of their inhabitants. No particular significance should be attached to small differences between estimates of two countries because of the margin of error inherent in the methods of estimation."

The grouping of countries, when not self-evident, is as follows:

Line 2: Northern and Western Europe includes Belgium, Denmark, Finland, France, Iceland, Ireland, Luxembourg, Netherlands, Norway, Sweden, United Kingdom, all, except Ireland, with per capita product well above $700.

Line 3: Other Europe includes Austria, West Germany (and West Berlin), Switzerland, Italy, and the group labeled "other" Europe in the *Yearbook*, with per capita income of $750 but only about 0.2 million of population.

Line 12: Less developed Europe includes Greece, Malta and Gozo, Cyprus (listed in the *Yearbook* under Asia), Portugal, and Spain.

Line 13: Latin America includes all countries in the Western Hemisphere except the United States and Canada.

Line 14: The Middle East includes Egypt (listed in the *Yearbook* under Africa), Aden, Iran, Iraq, Israel, Jordan, Lebanon, Muscat and Oman, Saudi-Arabia, Syria, Turkey, Yemen, and "other" Asia, which appears to be dominated by Kuwait and Bahrain.

Line 15: Asia is the total shown in the *Yearbook,* excluding Japan, Cyprus, and the Asian countries listed in the notes to line 14, plus the total shown for Oceania, excluding Australia and New Zealand (with 2.2 million of population).

Line 16: Africa is the total shown, excluding Egypt.

Communist Countries:

Line 7: For the U.S.S.R. Stanley Cohn in "The Gross National Product in the Soviet Union: Comparative Growth Rates," *Dimensions of Soviet Economic Power,* Joint Economic Committee, 87th Congress, 2nd Session (Washington, D.C., 1962), Part II, Table 4, p. 76, sets gross national product in 1960 at $193.6 billion, on the basis of IMF conversion rates (that is, those used for non-Communist countries), compared with $504.4 billion for the United States—which, with 214.4 and 180.7 million respectively for population (according to the United Nations, *Demographic Yearbook, 1962,* New York, 1963), yields a ratio of the U.S.S.R. per capita to the U. S. per capita of 0.32. Allowing a higher rate of growth in per capita product in the U.S.S.R. than in the United States from 1958 to 1960, we set the ratio for 1958 roughly at 0.30; which, multiplied by the per capita of $2,324 for the United States, yielded an estimate of $700 for the U.S.S.R. The population for the Soviet Union in 1958 was taken from James W. Brackett, "Demographic Trends and Population Policy in the Soviet Union," *Dimensions of Soviet Economic Power,* Table A-1, p. 555.

Line 8: Eastern Europe includes Albania, Bulgaria, Czechoslovakia, East Germany (and East Berlin), Hungary, Poland, Rumania, and Yugoslavia. Population totals for 1958 were taken from United Nations, *Demographic Yearbook, 1962,* Table 4, pp. 138ff. Product per capita, for the group as a whole, was estimated by relating it to that for the U.S.S.R. In United Nations, *Statistical Papers*, Ser. E, No. 1, entitled *National and Per Capita Incomes, Seventy Countries—1949* (New York, 1950), the average national income per capita for 1949 for Czechoslovakia, Hungary, Poland, and Yugoslavia combined was 88 percent of that for the U.S.S.R. (with the latter 21 percent of the one for the United States, a not unreasonable ratio when compared with 0.30 for 1958). The group excludes East Germany (which might raise its average) but also Bulgaria, Rumania, and Albania (which might lower its average). Setting the ratio for 1958 at 0.85 we derived a per capita of $600 for Communist Eastern Europe as a group.

Line 9: For Communist China, gross domestic product in 1957 prices was derived from T. C. Liu and K. C. Yeh, *The Economy of the Chinese Mainland: National Income and Economic Development, 1933-1959* (Rand Corporation Memorandum, RM-3519-Pr, April 1963, photo-offset; to be published by the Princeton University Press in 1964), I, 94-95, Tables 8 and 9. We converted it to 1957 U.S. prices by the rate of 2.617 yuan to $1 (*ibid.*, p. xxiv), and shifted it to 1958 prices by the price index implicit in U. S. gross national product estimates (see the *Yearbook of National Accounts Statistics, 1962*, p. 279). Population in 1957 is set at 637 million in Liu and Yeh, Table 24, p. 149, and at 643 million in the United Nations, *Economic Survey of Asia and the Far East, 1961* (Bangkok, 1962), p. 91, Table 3-14; we assumed 640 million for 1957 and 2.6 percent growth from 1957 to 1958.

Line 10: Other Communist countries in Asia include North Korea, North Vietnam, and Mongolia. Population was taken or estimated from the *Demographic Yearbook, 1962*, Table 4; and per capita product for the whole group was assumed to be the same as for Communist China—probably a substantial underestimate for Mongolia, but the latter accounted for only 0.9 million of the total of 26.7 million of population.

TABLE 2. DISTRIBUTION OF POPULATION AND OF GROSS DOMESTIC PRODUCT, GROUPS OF COUNTRIES BY PER CAPITA PRODUCT, 1958

	Non-Comm. Developed (1)	Communist (2)	Non-Communist Less Developed Total (3)	Latin America (4)	Middle East (5)	Asia (6)	Africa (7)	World Total (8)
1. Number of country units distinguished	22	4(13)	117	30	13	27	42	143(152)

A. ABSOLUTE TOTALS

POPULATION (MILLIONS)
Groups by per capita product:

	(1)	(2)	(3)	(4)	(5)	(6)	(7)	(8)
2. Under $100	0	681.7	827.7	7.6	6.6	679.8	133.7	1,509.4
3. $100 to 200	0	0	210.2	21.2	62.9	69.7	56.4	210.2
4. $200 to 400	0	0	254.4	137.8	27.9	13.1	28.5	254.4
5. $400 through 700	150.2	321.6	28.7	26.2	2.0	0	0	500.5
6. Over $700	400.6	0	8.2	6.9	1.3	0	0	408.8
7. Total, lines 2-6	550.8	1,003.3	1,329.2	199.7	100.7	762.6	218.6	2,883.3

GROSS DOMESTIC PRODUCT ($ BILLIONS)
Groups by per capita product:

	(1)	(2)	(3)	(4)	(5)	(6)	(7)	(8)
8. Under $100	0	48.4	54.8	0.7	0.3	44.5	9.2	103.2
9. $100 to 200	0	0	30.8	3.4	9.3	9.9	8.3	30.8
10. $200 to 400	0	0	69.4	37.2	5.7	3.3	9.0	69.4
11. $400 through 700	66.6	213.7	14.1	12.7	1.2	0	0	294.4
12. Over $700	653.1	0	6.1	4.9	1.2	0	0	659.2
13. Total, lines 8-12	719.7	262.1	175.2	58.9	17.7	57.7	26.5	1,157.0

[32]

TABLE 2. (continued)

B. PERCENTAGE DISTRIBUTION

POPULATION								
Groups by per capita product:								
14. Under $100	0	67.9	62.3	3.8	6.6	89.1	61.2	52.3
15. $100 to 200	0	0	15.8	10.6	62.5	9.1	25.8	7.3
16. $200 to 400	0	0	19.1	69.0	27.7	1.7	13.0	8.8
17. $400 through 700	27.3	32.1	2.2	13.1	2.0	0	0	17.4
18. Over $700	72.7	0	0.6	3.5	1.3	0	0	14.2
GROSS DOMESTIC PRODUCT								
Groups by per capita product:								
19. Under $100	0	18.5	31.3	1.2	1.7	77.1	34.7	8.9
20. $100 to 200	0	0	17.6	5.8	52.5	17.2	31.3	2.7
21. $200 to 400	0	0	39.6	63.1	32.2	5.7	34.0	6.0
22. $400 through 700	9.3	81.5	8.0	21.6	6.8	0	0	25.4
23. Over $700	90.7	0	3.5	8.3	6.8	0	0	57.0

NOTES

Underlying sources are given in the notes to Table 1.

The numbers in parentheses in line 1, columns 2 and 8, include all distinct countries in Communist Eastern Europe and in Communist Asia, other than China; but since Communist Eastern Europe and Communist Asia, excepting China, are each taken as a bloc, only four Communist units are distinguished. "Other" Africa, North America, South America, and so forth, are also treated as one bloc each, although they cover several distinct units.

TABLE 3. SELECTED ECONOMIC AND SOCIAL INDICATORS, COUNTRIES GROUPED
BY NATIONAL INCOME PER CAPITA, POST-WORLD WAR II YEARS

	Groups of Countries by Per Capita Income					
	$1,000 and over (1)	$575 to 1,000 (2)	$350 to 575 (3)	$200 to 350 (4)	$100 to 200 (5)	Under $100 (6)
1. Number of countries	6	11	14	13	14	10
2. Population (mill.)	216.7	396.8	183.8	226.2	171.5	667.4
Averages (unweighted arithmetic means)						
3. Per capita income, 1956-58 ($)	1,366	760	431	269	161	72
4. Per capita energy consumption, 1956-58 (kilogrammes of coal equivalent)	3,900	2,710	1,861	536	265	114
5. Percentage of male labor force in agriculture, 1956 (40 countries)	17.0	21.0	35.0	53.0	64.0	74.0
6. Percentage of national income originating in agriculture, latest year (42 countries)	11.4	10.9	15.3	29.9	33.4	40.8
7. Level of urbanization, around 1955	43	39	35	26	14	9
8. Per capita calorie consumption, latest year (40 countries)	3,153	2,944	2,920	2,510	2,240	2,070
9. Percentage of starchy staples in total calories, latest year (40 countries)	45.0	53.0	60.0	74.0	70.0	77.0

[34]

	Groups of Countries by Per Capita Income					
	$1,000 and over (1)	$575 to 1,000 (2)	$350 to 575 (3)	$200 to 350 (4)	$100 to 200 (5)	Under $100 (6)
0. Percentage of population, 15 years and over, illiterate, about 1950	2.0	6.0	19.0	30.0	49.0	71
1. Percentage of school enrollment to four-fifths of the 5-19 age group, latest year	91.0	84.0	75.0	60.0	48.0	37
2. Expectation of life at birth, 1955-58 (years)	70.6	67.7	65.4	57.4	50.0	41.7
3. Infant mortality rate per 1000, 1955-58	24.9	41.9	56.8	97.2	131.1	180.0

NOTES

Except for population, data are from United Nations, *Report on the World Social ituation* (New York, 1961), chap. III, Table 1, p. 41 and Table 5, pp. 47-49. Population is from the sources given for Table 1.

Lines 1 and 2: Number of countries and population for which national income is used. Unless otherwise indicated in the stub, the number of countries for other indexes is close to that in line 1.

Of world population, 2.88 billion (given in Table 1), 1.86 billion are covered here. The chief omissions are Mainland China (0.66 billion), most of the Middle East (only Israel is covered here), and most of Africa (only the Union of South Africa, Ghana, and the Congo are covered here).

Line 3: Conversion from domestic currency to U. S. dollars is by money exchange rates.

Line 4: Energy consumption refers to coal, coke and lignite, petroleum and its products, natural and manufactured gas and energy.

Line 7: Percentage of population in metropolitan areas of more than 100,000 inhabitants.

Line 11: Excludes pre-primary and higher education.

CHARACTERISTICS OF
MODERN ECONOMIC GROWTH

THE AIM of this and of the two lectures that follow is to evaluate post-World War II economic growth in all parts of the world for which data are available. But such an evaluation requires an historical perspective, some cognizance of the characteristics of modern economic growth over a long period—so that the recent experience can be seen as a segment of a longer past. This lecture, therefore, is devoted to a selective review of some major characteristics of the economic growth of nations in modern times. We also need to consider the impact of World War II, since that should at least suggest the reaction to be expected in the postwar period. The next lecture will be devoted to such a review of the relevant aspects of the World War II experience. It is only in the last lecture that we shall observe the pattern of economic growth in post-World War II years, and examine the various explanations that can be suggested.

In turning now to the characteristics of modern economic growth, we are, perforce, selective, for it is not possible, nor is it necessary, to review even briefly all significant features of the economic growth of nations since the late eighteenth or early nineteenth century. But even in such a selective review it is useful to distinguish between those characteristics of aggregate growth and structural change that can be observed

internally, within all or most of the nations that have participated in modern economic growth and which we now recognize as developed, and the characteristics that reflect the impact of modern economic growth in its international spread,
which affects the external relations among nations, developed
and underdeveloped. Therefore, we shall distinguish between
the intra-national and the international characteristics of modern economic growth; and deal with them separately.

2

In Table 4 we have a summary record of the aggregate
growth of total product, population, and per capita product
for fourteen countries, all of which are in the developed category (or close to it) and for which long-term records are available. A few more countries with equally long records (Australia, Argentina, Mexico) could be added, but the latter two are
not fully developed, and the record for the former raises questions that need not detain us here. While even more countries
with shorter records could be added, Table 4 is adequate for
the present purpose since it covers most of the developed
countries of the world and clearly illustrates the distinctive
feature of *aggregate* growth in modern times. The product
totals are either national income, net domestic product, gross
domestic product, net national product, or gross national product: the differences in their over-all rates for a long period are
minor.

The main features of aggregate growth suggested are the
familiar ones—the unusually high rates of growth of both population and per capita product. For the periods from the beginning of modern economic growth (that is, omitting 1700-80
for England and Wales, 1851-55 to 1871-75 for Germany, and
1861-65 to 1898-1902 for Italy), rates of growth of total product ranged from 20 to 50 percent per decade, implying multiplication of total output in a century to between 6 and 58

times; rates of population growth, except in France, ranged from 6 to over 20 percent per decade, implying multiplication of the population in a century to between 2 and over 6 times; and rates of growth of per capita product ranged from 14 to 30 percent per decade (excluding the average for the U.S.S.R., which is subject to an appreciable discount), implying multiplication over a century to between 3.7 and 14 times.

Allowing for various upward biases in the estimates of product (but not of population), which, however, should be offset by failures to reflect improvements in quality of many complex products of modern technology, and for the downward biases in the use of recent price relations as weights, the rates of growth just cited are unusually high, in that they are far higher than rates of increase of population and per capita product observed in the preceding centuries, or in those countries which until recently had not managed to take advantage of the potentials of modern economic growth. In England and Wales, Germany, and Italy, for which the records go back before the beginning of industrialization, the earlier rises in per capita product in particular are much lower than in the later decades of growth. We also know from a variety of evidence and from backward projection, that the rates of population growth associated with the modern period, and found until most recently only in the developed countries, are, if conservatively set between 6 and 10 percent per decade, at least ten times higher than they were in the centuries preceding the mid-eighteenth century. A similar variety of evidence suggests that the rates of increase in per capita product, characteristic of the developed countries from the beginning of their participation in the process of modern development, must be high multiples of the rates of growth (if the latter were positive) in the earlier centuries: the average levels of per capita product in the most advanced countries of today just before their entry into the modern growth process were, at best, two to four times above the bare minimum of subsistence—a factor lower than that produced by modern economic growth in most countries in a single century.

The high rate of growth of per capita product is of greater interest to us here than that of population. Yet, the acceleration in population growth and, particularly, the shape it took in modern times are important in explaining the rise in productivity that lay behind the rise in per capita income. Anticipating a later reference to the impact of population growth in the post-World War II period, we note here that the population "explosion" is not something new but has a relatively long history in the developed parts of the world, and even in those underdeveloped areas that have been under the influence of the developed nations for some time.

But the rise in per capita product is the most conspicuous single characteristic of modern economic growth. And, in looking for the force behind it, we find that this rise was attained with no apparent great rise in inputs per capita—at least, when the latter are measured in simple, conventional, but nevertheless significant, terms. As far as labor input is concerned, evidence for several developed countries indicates that the proportion of labor force to population tended to rise (from the mid-nineteenth to the mid-twentieth century), but by relatively limited fractions; and even that trend is observable only for labor force excluding unpaid family members in agriculture. By contrast, average hours per worker, under conditions of full employment, tended to decline substantially —roughly between a fifth and a third over the last century. The combination of these two trends produced a *downward* movement in man-hours per capita, of about 2 percent per decade for the thirteen developed countries for which the underlying data are available. This means that the rise in per capita product, ranging between 14 and 30 percent per decade, cannot be assigned to a rise in labor input per capita, at least in terms of man-hours—whatever may be said of the quality, skill, and education of labor; and that the rate of growth in product per man-hour would be two to three percentage points higher than the decadal rate of growth in product per capita.

Of course, reproducible material capital grew rapidly; and the rate of growth of total material capital must also have been high. Consequently, the input of capital per head of population must have increased, and thus contributed to the rise in total product per capita. The available data, for only a few countries (Great Britain, Belgium, the United States, Australia, and Japan, with partial data for Norway, Germany, and Argentina), indicate that the average ratio of *total* capital to total output declined roughly a fifth over the long period of between a half and a full century—although in one or two of the countries the *reproducible* capital output ratio increased. This suggests that whatever the percentage rise per decade in total product per head of population, the decadal rise in total capital per head was a fifth lower. The basic weight of the contribution of material capital to output can be set at 0.25, in accordance with the usual share of income from property (or capital) in total national income, the remaining 0.75 being assigned to labor or man-hours. (The allocation could be 0.30 and 0.70 or 0.80 and 0.20 without materially affecting the results.) If per capita product rose, say, 20 percent per decade, man-hours per capita declined about 2 percent per decade, and material capital per head rose 16 percent per decade (a fifth lower than product per head), then, in a century, product per head would grow from 100 to 619; the contribution of material capital (weighted 0.25) would grow from 25 to 110; the contribution of man-hours, held at fixed initial factor costs, would change from 75 to (75×0.82), or 62; the total contribution of capital and labor inputs to the rise in per capita product would be ($110 + 62 - 100$), or 72, out of a total rise in per capita product of (619 — 100), or 519, or less than a seventh. While the parameters can be modified, it is clear that if labor input is measured by man-hours unweighted by skill and education, and we deal with total, not reproducible, material capital, and assign to total capital input the proportional weight suggested by the share of pure property incomes in total product, the contribution of any rise in *inputs* per capita to the growth of total product per capita will be limited, ranging from less than a seventh to not much more than a fifth. In other words, by far the major proportion of the remarkable long-term rise in per capita product in the course of modern economic growth must be attributed either to changes in skill, education, and so on, of the labor force, or to other sources of the large increase in productivity per man-hour combined with a unit of material capital—and not to any increase in inputs per head.[1]

The broad conclusions to the effect that the enormous increase in per capita product, which characterizes modern economic growth, is largely the result of a rise in efficiency, that is, output per unit of input, when the latter are simply man-hours and material capital, has become familiar: it has been corroborated by several studies, particularly for this country, by Abramovitz, Kendrick, Denison, and others.[2] It

---

[1] The conclusion may not apply to some exceptional cases and periods, such as the U.S.S.R. between 1928 and 1940, where the proportional contribution of inputs was much greater. Also this is, of course, a statistical allocation and neglects the possible effects of the rise in scale, represented by the growth in the absolute volume of total inputs. But the scale effects may themselves be dependent upon growth in the stock of technological and organizational knowledge, the source also of increasing productivity expressed as a rise in output per unit of input. If so, references to scale effects are again references to supply of knowledge; not to any specific properties of the absolute volume of inputs.

[2] For the United States see Moses Abramovitz, Resource and Output Trends in the United States since 1870, *Occasional Paper* 52, National Bureau of Economic Research, New York, 1956; Robert Solow, "Technical Change and the Aggregate Production Function," *Review of Economics and Statistics*, August 1957; John W. Kendrick, *Productivity*

has, naturally, led to greater attention to investment in human beings, changes in quality and education of the labor force, changes in organization of economic units, and other observable sources of the rise in efficiency; and much valuable new work on the investment in education and in training on the job has been done, largely by Schultz, Becker, and Mincer.[3] And it is also reflected in current policy relating to education and research and development expenditures. One hardly needs to stress the point further that the sources of increasing per capita product in modern economic growth are the stock of technological knowledge that has been accumulated, partly on the basis of expanded scientific and related knowledge; the variety of social inventions, devices necessary to accommodate the new tools and technology; and the capacity of human beings, as individuals and members of society, not only to create such knowledge but to serve as its carriers and appliers. But, with the emphasis in recent studies on costs and returns of education and training on the job, and quantitative weights to be assigned to such aspects of increased efficiency as economies of scale, the changing content of education and training and the changes in the stock of knowledge that affect economies of scale should not be overlooked. A medieval craftsman, in his apprenticeship to become a full-fledged member of the guild, spent perhaps as many years in education and training on the job as a member of a modern profession; and a mature medieval farmer probably spent more years in training and acquiring competence than a graduate

Trends in the United States, Princeton, NBER, 1961; and Edward F. Denison, The Sources of Economic Growth in the United States and the Alternatives Before Us, *CED Supplementary Paper no. 13,* New York, 1960; for Norway see Odd Aukrust and Juul Bjerke, "Real Capital and Economic Growth in Norway, 1900-56," in Raymond Goldsmith and Christopher Saunders, eds., *Income and Wealth,* Series VIII, London, 1959.

[3] See *The Journal of Political Economy,* vol. LXX, no. 5, part 2 (*October 1962*), papers on Investment in Human Beings.

of a modern agricultural school. But, despite the eventual contribution of these experienced and skilled members of the medieval community to the evolution of science and modern technology, it would be difficult to argue that their productivity even approached, let alone surpassed, the productivity of the average member of the labor force in a modern economic society. The crucial difference is not so much in the time and energy put into education and training, but in the basic content of that training—the underlying capacity of the knowledge transmitted to control production processes, the emergence of experimental science and the empirical outlook which, building upon past attainments of mankind, provided the indispensable basis for modern economic growth. Likewise, scale differences existed in pre-modern times, as comparisons of pre-modern industries and types of productive tasks reveal; but the functional relations between efficiency and scale are largely a product, and indeed an integral component, of technological knowledge.

In particular connection with the further discussion of the impact of World War II and its aftermath, several aspects of the association between the increased stock of useful knowledge and the striking rise in per capita product and per unit efficiency of modern economic growth deserve explicit mention. First, the increase in productive power by which the supply of economic goods per head was raised, could also be used for a changed and intensified technology of warfare—a point that scarcely needs elaboration. Second, the attainment of high per capita product meant that a smaller proportion of output was represented by prime necessities, and, correspondingly, a smaller proportion of total resources was devoted to their production. By contrast, the accumulated capital, in the form of producer goods and consumers' nonperishable commodities (particularly the durable) grew apace, providing large reserves that could be used more intensively in times of emergency. As a result, the greatly increased per capita product in peacetime meant that during wartime total output could decline to relatively low proportions without life and warfare coming to a stop because of the sheer impossibility of continuing. Third, much of the stock of useful knowledge, of the complex of available technology, material and social, unlike the material capital that embodies it, is indestructible so long as a sufficient proportion of the population, equipped with the necessary education, skill, and patterns of social behavior, remains to carry on and rebuild after the destruction of war. It will be observed later that one factor in the rapid economic recovery in the developed nations after World War II was this reliance of modern economic performance on the stock of useful knowledge, which, in its overt, rigorous expression in a variety of forms, in multiple storage depositories—libraries, laboratories, plants, and offices, or in the variety of its human carriers—is not susceptible to fatal destruction—even in the intensive warfare exemplified by World War II. This, of course, does not mean that similar resistance and survival will be possible in a future major war with its threat of "total" devastation.

3

If a high rate of growth of per capita product, accompanied by a high growth rate of per unit efficiency, is one basic characteristic of modern economic growth observed within the developed nations, the second is a high rate of structural shifts. These are changes in the shares of various industries in output, labor force, or the stock of material capital; in the position of people in the labor force, as between entrepreneurial and self-employed workers, on one hand, and employees, on the other, with a variety of occupations cutting across industry lines; in the shares of the private and the government sectors, and of various types of business unit within the former, the particularly important distinction being between the large impersonal corporations and the small individual firms; in the patterns of life associated with rising per capita income and attachment to different industries, reflected in the allocation between savings and consumption and of the latter among various categories of consumer goods; in the factoral and size distribution of income; in the composition and relative importance of exports and imports, and hence in the nature of international economic relations.

These structural shifts occur because the impact of technological changes is not felt equally or simultaneously by all industries, but rather results in the continuous creation of new industries and obsolescence of old; and because, with the increase in per capita product, the demand for some goods, while still growing, may rise less than the demand for other goods. And these shifts in industrial structure, which reflect the combined effects of the differential impact of technological change and the rise in per capita income, in turn induce changes in related aspects: industrialization—that is, the movement away from the agricultural sector—leads to urbanization, shifts in scale of economic plants and firms, and changes in employment status and in the structure of income allocation. Because material and social technology has been changing rapidly and because per capita product has been increasing rapidly, the rate of structural shifts within the national economies that have participated in modern economic growth has also been high.

In the present connection, we are concerned with those aspects of structural shifts that bear directly upon the roles of individuals within the economy, the implicit high rates of their mobility, and the effects which these shifts, combined with the rapid growth of population, may have upon the basic pattern of political organization of countries participating in modern economic growth, the nation-states.

Table 5 suggests the magnitude of one important structural shift, the trend away from agriculture, in its impact on the distribution of the total labor force between the A and the non-A sectors. Over the relatively long periods covered, the shortest being the three decades for the U.S.S.R., the share of the labor force attached to the A sector declined sharply in each of the thirteen countries; and the share attached to the non-A sector rose correspondingly. By comparing the decadal rate of proportional decline in the A sector share and of proportional rise in the non-A sector share (columns 5 and 6) with the approximate rate of growth of the total labor force (column 7) we can estimate the percentage rate of change in absolute numbers attached to the two major sectors. Thus, in Great Britain, total labor force grew roughly 10 percent per decade; the share of the A sector declined 12.6 percent per decade; and the share of the non-A sector grew 2.0 percent per decade. Hence, the rate of change in the number attached to the A sector was $(1.10 \times 0.874) - 1$, or a decline of 3.9 percent per decade; whereas the rate of growth of the number attached to the non-A sector was $(1.10 \times 1.02) - 1$, or 12.2 percent per decade. By this calculation, of the thirteen countries in Table 5, four (Great Britain, France, Belgium, and Sweden) show declines over the period in the number attached to the A sector, and four (Switzerland, Denmark, Italy, and the U.S.S.R.) show little change—so that the impressive growth in total labor force is concentrated in the non-A sector; and in the remaining five countries, the decadal rate of growth in number attached to the A sector ranged from 1.5 to 5.9 percent. By contrast, the rate of growth of number attached to the non-A sector ranged, if we exclude the low 6.2 percent for France and the very high 55.4 percent for the U.S.S.R., between 7.5 percent (for Belgium) and 35.9 percent (for the United States).

The implication of the large volume of internal migration and mobility suggested by the evidence of Table 5 is of primary interest here. The growth of the labor force is a result partly of the rate of natural increase of the population (that is, excess of birth over death rates); partly of the net balance of external migration (that is, excess of immigration over emigration rates); and partly of the ratio of labor force to total population, reflecting changing or different propensities to enter or remain in the labor force. Of these three determinants, the natural increase rate is by far the most important in most countries, although in some—the United States, Canada, and, to a lesser degree, Italy—external migration was significant through most of the period covered in Table 5. If we assume, to simplify the illustration, that the rate of growth of the labor force, as affected by the three determinants noted above, is the same for the components attached to the A and non-A sectors, the net internal migration necessary to produce the trends shown in Table 5 can be calculated. Thus for Great Britain, the labor force attached to the A sector would have increased, without migration, 10 percent per decade. In fact, it declined 3.9 percent per decade. Thus in the first decade, when the initial share of the labor force attached to the A sector was 0.25, the rise without migration would have amounted to (0.25×0.10), or 2.5 percent of the total labor force (at the initial date); and the actual decline amounted to (0.25×0.039), or 1 percent (at the initial date). Needed internal migration was thus 3.5 percent of the total labor force at the beginning of the decade (or 3.5/110, or 3.2 percent, of the total labor force at the end of the decade). A similar calculation for the U.S.S.R. in the first decade (1928-38) suggests a net movement that amounted to 15.0 percent of the total labor force at the beginning of the decade (and 12.3 percent of the total at the end).

Shifts of some 3 to 12 percent of the total labor force over a decade may seem at first glance small. But even such small shifts mean that all, or almost all, of the natural increase of a large proportion of the economic community (that in the A sector) do not have the same industrial attachment as their parents; and that much of the increase of the labor force in the growing sectors consists of in-migrants from elsewhere. The volume of such migration is amplified, in this particular case, by the higher natural increase rates of rural and hence of agricultural population than of the urban and nonagricultural population. But two other considerations emphasize the importance of the process in its full magnitude and perspective.

First, the shift in the distribution between the A and non-A sectors is only one of many that accompany modern economic growth. There are shifts even within the A sector proper and, of course, among the significantly different subsectors within the large non-A sector—such as manufacturing, diverse service industries, and so forth. There are, in addition, shifts among occupations, economic status positions, and the like, all cutting across industrial sector lines and proceeding at fairly rapid rates. A fully articulated distribution of the labor force, distinguishing all the cells that are significantly different with respect to the character and location of the economic role involved, would reveal far more changes in percentage shares than are indicated in Table 5—and correspondingly imply far more mobility—so long as the natural increase differentials (to use the most important determinant) are not correlated (or, as is more likely, are negatively correlated) with the rate of growth differentials in the component cells distinguished.[4]

---

[4] The differences in natural increase among economic groups (standardized for age and sex) in the countries that we are considering are largely a matter of differences in birth rates, the death rates displaying small absolute disparities. High birth rates tend to characterize rural areas and other groups within the economy not yet affected by modern economic growth and, in general, the more traditional segments in

Second, from the actual changes in the distribution of the labor force by industry, occupation, location, and so on, and the distributions based on known rates of increase (natural and other, except for migration) of groups within some initial distribution, we can derive only *net* migration, and not the gross flows in which the movement of an individual from *a* to *b* is *not* offset by the movement of another individual from *b* to *a*. The volume of net migration is smaller than that of gross, if only because differential economic opportunities may attract some migrants who do not succeed in making the adjustment and leave; and because in any economic society there are nuclei of opportunities even within declining or slowly growing sectors and nuclei of obsolescence within growing sectors. It is only reasonable to assume that if the volume of net economic mobility or migration generated in the course of modern economic growth is large, the volume of gross migration is much larger.

If the rapid structural shifts mean large volumes of mobility and migration in space and, within the economic structure, personal or intergenerational mobility, they also mean more rapid rises in the economic level of the groups attached to the dynamic rapidly growing sectors during a given period, and corresponding declines in the relative economic level of groups attached to the increasingly obsolescent and slowly growing sectors. And these shifts in relative position, accompanied by extensive mobility and migration, occur under conditions of rapidly growing population and urbanization. All three complexes of trends seem to me to require a greater role of government in modern economic growth; and to intensify the nation-oriented basis of consensus for this in-

---

which the economic growth potentials are probably lower. Hence, for a long period, while the lower birth rate pattern spreads from the larger cities and the more highly professionalized occupations to others, the natural increase differentials and the differential rates of growth within the labor force will be negatively associated.

creased role. While the connections indicated are hazardous conjectures, their importance warrants an explicit statement of some speculative suggestions.

The economic mobility of a large part of the population, which involves spatial and social detachment from the family and place of origin, and movement to the anonymous and market-oriented environment of the larger cities, should weaken traditional and family ties; and, in general, shift orientation from the smaller to the larger community. The weakening of family and small community ties necessitates a shift of values and a search for a basis of consensus that can be found in the larger communities to which an increasing proportion of population gravitates. And since religious and other supranational bonds are also loosened as a result of the secularization that accompanies, and is in a sense indispensable for, modern economic growth, such consensus is found in the nation's unity and independence, in the sovereign nation-state as the carrier of the common and distinctive values of the wider society.

This consensus centered on the nation-state is both required for, and enhanced by, the proliferation of society-wide problems generated by modern economic growth with which only the nation-state is capable of dealing. It has been increasingly realized that, given the large potential of economic growth embodied in modern technology, the major problem, particularly for the societies that lag behind in the utilization of this potential (and all countries, except the single pioneer, lag at some time or other), is to modify institutions and patterns of behavior inherited from the past in order to make growth possible. Since the impact of this modification was different for different groups, and was thus productive of internal conflicts, only a central sovereign government reflecting an adequate consensus could assume the responsibility. Furthermore, the course of modern economic growth itself, with its continuous shifts in relative position, problems of scale, and so on, generated problems and conflicts that could be dealt with only by a central government that was empowered to make decisions—ranging from those on the public domain, on the basic rules for the operation of the markets in goods, resources, or claims, on the one hand, to those on the more specific concerns of health, safety, or traffic mobility of the urbanized population masses, on the other. The nation-state has always been important in modern economic growth in defining the overriding conditions of economic activity; but its concerns have become increasingly diversified and pervasive, as modern economic growth has proceeded, partly because of the rise in scale and the intensification of frictions for which market mechanisms provided no effective solution; and partly because of the greater demand by society, with the greater mobility and detachment of individuals from the small and more traditionally organized communities, that government assume responsibility for additional tasks that previously may have been neglected or handled by other means.

Thus, there is ground for assuming that the problems generated by the rise in scale and by structural shifts characteristic of modern economic growth intensified the role of the nation-state and of its government. This, of course, affected international relations; and the latter in turn affected the role and functions of government within the nation-state. We now turn to an explicit discussion of some of the international aspects of modern economic growth.

4

The international impact of modern economic growth relevant to our theme can be discussed under five heads: (a) the increase in accessibility of various parts of the world, associated with major technological changes in transport and communication; (b) the rapid growth in the stock of useful material and social technology, which is a worldwide potential; (c) the spread, at different times, of modern economic growth to an increasing number of economies, several of them large; (d) the wide differences in the rate of aggregate growth, and hence the rapid shifts in economic power among the developed countries, and still more between the developed and underdeveloped; (e) the spread of the network of international economic flows, combined with the restrictive effects of the divisive tendencies due to the increasing diversity of political organization.

(a) The technological revolution connected with modern economic growth in the field of transport and communication has been most conspicuous and needs no elaborate demonstration. The introduction of steam railroads solved the problem of transport of men and commodities over land that had been a long-standing difficulty in most economies. The further development of transport and the recent burgeoning of modern communication devices are familiar trends. As a result, practically all the world, for the first time in history, was open to relatively easy linkages and flows, both material and spiritual. The development of worldwide accessibility naturally was only permitted, not forced, by modern technology, but the latter was a necessary, if not sufficient, condition.

Needless to say, these changes in transport and communication facilities also affected the internal organization of nations. In particular, they permitted those nation-states that, by some combination of historical events, organized large populations on large areas within a single political framework, to strengthen the links among various regions to attain effective unity and easy mobility within their boundaries at no danger to their power in external policy. This meant that the entry into modern economic development of the large nations, usually possessed of large land areas, could be accompanied by an increase in internal unity and accretion of power vis-à-vis the rest of the world.

(b) As obvious as the technological revolution in transport and communication is the rapid growth in the stock of useful knowledge that is the basis either for a powerful material technology or for the social institutions and devices that provide the proper auspices for the new tools and production methods. Since we cannot, in the present state of our knowledge, express this stock in meaningful quantitative terms, or even give some definitive shape to the factors that determine its rate of growth, we must rely on impressions and suggestive details rather than on hard data in asserting that its growth was rapid. But the progress of science and its diversification into specialized but related disciplines, the increasing proportion of modern production that represents a technology that has originated only within the last century, and the many social and economic institutions that are also of recent origin—all imply a marked upward trend in the stock of useful technological and social knowledge.

Moreover, this knowledge has become embodied in forms that are available to the world at large, in the sense that it is valid anywhere under the specified conditions, can be learned by anyone who is interested, and is geared to needs that are practically universal. This statement should not be taken to mean that all such knowledge is equally accessible; nor does it deny some bias toward the problems and interests of the developed countries which were the locus of its origin and growth in the recent centuries. But, by and large, the tools, material and intellectual, that it provides, and the vast accumulation of empirical knowledge on which these are based and which permit their use, are available and valuable to the less developed countries also, despite the additions the latter must make in the way of knowledge of their own specific conditions and of adaptation of the technology to fit these conditions.

(c) The entry at *different* times by different countries into modern economic growth, the beginning of economic modernization, revealed by a sustained and high rate of growth of total and per capita product, and by such associated structural shifts as industrialization and urbanization, is an historical fact of overshadowing importance. The world would be quite different today if this were not true; if, for example, all the countries in the world at the end of the eighteenth century had embarked on economic modernization at about the same time—say, within one or two decades, and proceeded at the characteristic rates. Instead, Great Britain entered this process in the last quarter of the eighteenth century; the United States and perhaps France in the 1840's; Germany not fully until the 1870's; Japan in the late 1880's and perhaps more definitely in the 1890's; Italy not until the beginning of the twentieth century; Russia, after a slow start in the 1890's, not until the U.S.S.R. phase of the 1930's; and China is making strenuous efforts at a beginning in the 1960's. The same spread over time is applicable to economic modernization in the smaller countries.

The factors behind this differential timing of the initiation of modern economic growth, the sequential entry of nations in a kind of queue, cannot be discussed here: they lie presumably in the wide differences in historical heritage and in the resulting economic and social conditions, in the degree of preparedness. Here we are concerned with the consequences, of which the major one is the differences among nations in the rates of growth of product and hence of economic power. But before we turn to this result of sequential entry into economic modernization, three other aspects should be noted.

First, there is some semblance, in the sequence, of increasing departure from the original modern economic growth pattern in the Western European civilization of which the pioneer, Great Britain, was a member, as were all other major country followers until the last quarter of the nineteenth century.[5] With the emergence of Japan and Russia the focus shifted away from the Western European origins, and this shift would be accelerated if China and India were to follow. Corresponding to the increasing deviation of historical heritage of the later entrants from the originally conditioning civilization of the pioneer and early followers is a marked change in the social and political forms that economic modernization assumes.

Second, it should be stressed, relevant to our later discussion of World War II, that the spread of modern economic growth meant the emergence of several large and developed nations; and it is the participation of the large and developed nations that makes for a major war—major in the volume of resources that is devoted to war, in the advanced technology that is employed, and in the prolongation of designed destruction that is possible. When only one large nation is developed, the conditions for a major war do not exist, unless one assumes unrealistically the close union of a number of less developed countries; or unless a situation evolves, like that in the late eighteenth and early nineteenth centuries in the French and Napoleonic wars, where Great Britain, smaller but more economically developed, faced France, larger, politically modernized, but economically less developed. The century of peace that followed was terminated partly because the strains and tensions among the *several* large and developed nations had time to cumulate.

Third, Table 4 suggests that the later the entry into eco-

---

[5] For some deviant features in Germany, see Thorstein Veblen, *Imperial Germany and the Industrial Revolution*, New York, 1915.

nomic modernization, the higher the rate of economic growth tends to be, over the several decades past the initial date. The rates of growth of per capita product for the United States, Germany, and France are above those for Great Britain–United Kingdom, and those of Japan and the U.S.S.R. are particularly high. The rates of growth of total product follow much the same pattern except for France (with low rates because of population growth) and Italy. There is some danger in overstressing this association between date of entry and level of growth rates, since there are so few large countries and the estimates are subject to error; and yet such an association is not surprising since follower countries can take advantage of the large reservoir of untapped potential available, and are under strong pressures to achieve true independence and avoid a delay fraught with danger. At any rate, the association, and the resulting acceleration over time of the growth rates of successive entrants, can be accepted as a tentative conclusion.

(d)   The differences among nations in rates of growth of total product, population, and per capita product can be usefully distinguished between those among countries within the developed group, and those between developed countries on the one hand and the underdeveloped on the other. The former reflect the differences in the dates of entry into economic modernization. At the time that country A enters the process and country B is still not ready to begin, there will be marked differences between the rates of growth of the two in favor of country A; then when country B enters the process, its rates of growth may well exceed that of country A, particularly if, as frequently happens, the rate of population growth in A begins to decline after the original population "swarming." In the comparison of developed and underdeveloped countries, however, the differences in rates of growth will tend to persist, since by definition the former group comprises all those in which high rates of growth have been sustained and cumulative.[6]

In this connection the major point worth stressing is that when the average growth rate is high, as it is for product, population, and per capita income in modern economic growth, the differentials can also be absolutely large; and absolutely large differentials can produce rapid shifts in relative magnitudes of two countries. For example, if countries A and B start with equal products and the rate of growth in country A rises to double that of country B, an average rate of about 30 percent per decade might mean a 40 percent rate of rise in country A and a 20 percent rate in country B—in which case the product of country A will be 50 percent higher than that of country B in 2.6 decades; whereas with an average rate of 10 percent per decade and, say, 13.3 and 6.7 percent respectively for countries A and B, a differential of 50 percent would be attained only after 6.8 decades.

Two inferences are suggested by these observations. First, rapid shifts in economic magnitude, and perhaps economic power, generated by modern economic growth, are productive of strains among those nations that participate in the process, if political recognition of these changes in the balance of power is delayed and later claimed by threats of force. The drive for such political recognition—a greater share of influence in the less developed countries, with special treaties and privileges; expansion of territory at the expense of weaker neighbors; or recovery of losses sustained in the pre-growth past—may readily lead to war in an effort to demonstrate in a hard contest that the balance of power had shifted. Many wars in the second half of the nineteenth and in the early twentieth century, appear to have been due indirectly to shifts in economic and related power, beginning with those of Prussia and Germany (against Denmark, Austria, and

---

[6] See the discussion in the first lecture.

France); going on to the wars of Japan (with China and Russia); and concluding most recently with the China-India skirmish. It is reasonable to assume that such strains were also contributory causes of the two world wars.[7]

Second, changes in differentials in economic and related power between developed and underdeveloped countries have obviously been marked. The wide discrepancies among countries in per capita product, discussed in the first lecture, are due to a greater extent to the high rates of increase characteristic of modern economic growth in the developed countries, than to any initial pre-modernization differences in favor of the presently developed countries, although the latter were substantial. And this despite the distinct possibility, untestable except in a few cases, that the impact of the developed countries upon the underdeveloped has served to raise, not lower, the per capita income in the latter—so long as internal peace and some stability were maintained. For the contact did bring some elements of modernization and higher productivity to the underdeveloped areas along with an expanded foreign trade. The effect was limited, however, and was partly offset by the failure to induce the changes in the economic and social institutions required for far-reaching modernization; by limits imposed upon entrepreneurs and elites within these countries, particularly those with colonial status, that prevented the cumulation of self-generated, transforming decisions.

(e) The closer contact of different parts of the world with each other and the spread of economic modernization to an increasing number of countries should have made for greater

---

[7] This association between shifts in economic power and international strains possibly leading to wars has been emphasized by Ralph G. Hawtrey in *Economics of Sovereignty*, London, 1930 and 1952. The statements in the text do not pretend to ascribe all wars to this source, but merely suggest that the latter was significant in several wars and contributes greatly to international tensions.

international economic flows—of commodities, funds, and even of men (in international migration). Given the desire of countries participating in modern economic growth for natural resources and similar commodities available beyond their boundaries, and given their power to impose upon the possessors of these resources rules of trade and other economic behavior that would make such resources available, the expansion of foreign trade (and related financing flows) in particular should have been expected.

And, indeed, international economic flows did expand. A few figures relating to the volume of foreign commodity trade illustrate this trend.[8] Between 1850 and 1880 the rate of growth of world trade was 47 percent per decade; between 1876-80 and 1911-13 it was 39 percent per decade. For the period 1850-1900, world population is estimated to have grown between 6.5 and 7.5 percent per decade, and the growth from 1900 to 1910 was probably close to the higher figure. Hence world foreign trade *per capita* over the period 1850-1910 must have grown between 29 and 37 percent per decade. These rates are much higher than the rates of growth in per capita product in the developed countries in Table 4, which were mostly below 20 percent; and the rest of the world did not enjoy similar rises in per capita product. Despite the fact that the developed countries as a group accounted for a rising proportion of world population, the rate of growth of per capita product for the world as a

[8] For 1850 to 1880 the estimates of world volume of foreign trade in commodities cited in this and the next paragraph are from Loreto M. Dominguez, *International Trade, Industrialization and Economic Growth* (Pan American Union, mimeo., 1953), Table 4, p. 61. These are based on Mulhall's data, adjusted for price changes by the Jevons and Warren-Pearson price indexes. For 1876-1938 the estimates are based on Folke Hilgert, *Industrialization and Foreign Trade* (League of Nations, 1945), p. 157; and they were brought to 1947-51 by Dominguez. The estimates of world population are from the United Nations, *The Determinants and Consequences of Population Trends*, New York, 1953 and the recent *Demographic Yearbooks*.

whole could not have been much above 5 percent per decade (the developed countries throughout the period accounted for no more than a tenth of the world population). It follows that during this period, which could easily be extended back to 1820 with the same result, the proportion of world foreign trade to total world output must have risen markedly—and that for the less developed countries even more, since their total output was growing more slowly than that of the developed countries while their participation in the network of world trade was increasing. This statement concerning the more than proportional expansion of international trade flows is applicable, with some modifications, to the international flows of funds and men: the three-quarters of a century preceding World War I witnessed the emergence of a large international flow of capital funds and a volume of voluntary, economically responsive, international migration (primarily for Europe, the Western Hemisphere, and Oceania; and considerably more restricted for Asia and Africa) far larger than any observed in the earlier centuries, even in proportion to the base populations involved.

These trends toward widening international economic flows of a peaceful type, in increasing proportion to rising domestic volumes, were suspended and, indeed, reversed between World War I and the early 1950's. Here again the world foreign trade volumes tell the story clearly. Between 1911-13 and 1926-30 the volume grew 9 percent per decade and between 1926-30 and 1947-51, 12 percent per decade— although in both periods, unlike the earlier ones, these average ratios conceal the severe declines during the two wars and the depression of the 1930's and the sharp recoveries from them. Over the same periods, world population grew at almost the same rates—about 9 percent from 1910 to 1930, and 11.6 percent from 1930 to 1950. Hence, at best, per capita world trade was constant from about 1910 to about 1950, whereas per capita product must have continued to grow (it did in the increasing number of developed countries, and could hardly have declined significantly in the underdeveloped countries). If we assume, as a reasonable guess, a minimum rate of increase for world per capita product of 5 percent per decade, the total rise over the four decades would be over 20 percent; and the implication is that the proportion of world foreign trade to world output declined about a fifth—instead of rising markedly, as it did from 1850 (or 1820) to World War I. And this reversal occurred despite the increasing efficiency in transport and communication, and despite the rapid growth in the worldwide stock of useful knowledge that should have effected more intensive international division of labor and hence growing trade proportions. There were similar reversals in the trends in international flows of funds and men.

Such reversals were clearly due to the cumulation of divisive elements and strains, themselves partly due to the differential impact of modern economic growth on nations, which, perhaps in combination with other factors, brought on World War I, the dislocations that were its aftermath, and World War II. It shall be assumed here that these dislocations and the general pattern of the inter-war period are fairly well known—particularly as they apply to the developed countries in Europe and the Western Hemisphere, the deformations of political and economic structure in Nazi Germany, Fascist Italy, and militarized Japan, and the emergence of an autarkic dictatorial planned economy in the U.S.S.R. In this lecture, the aim is only to indicate the characteristics of modern economic growth in their long-term aspects that could provide the broad framework, rather than the detailed account, needed to understand the divided world economic structure, with the potentials of growth that it could generate, that existed on the eve of World War II.

One concluding comment: Both in this and in the preceding lecture we dwelt on the association between the role of the nation-state in providing conditions for modern economic growth within the society that it organizes, and its possible militancy in external relations, particularly in the early phases of its rapid growth. This emphasis may lead to the impression that such an association is indispensable, and that the external militancy and aggression is a necessary price to be paid for internal efficiency. Let me conclude by urging that while this association seems to be a roughly valid description of the past, it is not logically or analytically indispensable. In a different climate of views on national interest, in a world in which policies of aggression are ruled out by other views of the relation of man to man, no such association would be feasible; and the consensus for internal policy would not be grounded even in part on hostility, implicit or overt, to some other part of the world. The possible sources of internal consensus are numerous and are not limited to internationally divisive views; and it is the historically prevalent notions, not the analytically indispensable antecedents, that explain the association.

TABLE 4. GROWTH OF NATIONAL PRODUCT, POPULATION, AND PER CAPITA PRODUCT, SELECTED COUNTRIES, LONG PERIODS

	Duration of Period (years) (1)	Rate of Growth per Decade(%)			Coefficient of Multiplication in a Century		
		Total product (2)	Population (3)	Product per capita (4)	Total product (5)	Population (6)	Product per capita (7)
England and Wales–United Kingdom							
1. 1700 to 1780	80	5.3	3.2	2.0	1.7	1.4	1.2
2. 1780 to 1881	100	28.2	13.1	13.4	12.0	3.4	3.5
3. 1855-59 to 1957-59	101	21.1	6.1	14.1	6.8	1.8	3.7
France							
4. 1841-50 to 1960-62	105.5	20.8	2.5	17.9	6.6	1.3	5.2
Germany–West Germany							
5. 1851-55 to 1871-75	20	17.6	7.7	9.2			
6. 1871-75 to 1960-62	88	31.1	11.2	17.9	15.0	2.9	5.2
Netherlands							
7. 1900-04 to 1960-62	59	29.7	14.3	13.5	13.5	3.8	3.5
Belgium							
8. 1880 to 1960-62	80	22.2	6.4	14.8	7.5	1.9	4.0
Switzerland							
9. 1890-99 to 1957-59	63.5	25.7	8.3	16.1	9.8	2.2	4.4
Denmark							
10. 1870-74 to 1960-62	89	31.8	10.4	19.4	15.8	2.7	5.9
Norway							
11. 1865-74 to 1960-62	91.5	29.0	8.4	19.0	12.7	2.2	5.7
Sweden							
12. 1861-65 to 1960-62	98	36.9	6.7	28.3	23.2	1.9	12.1
Italy							
13. 1861-65 to 1898-1902	37	9.7	6.8	2.7			
14. 1898-1902 to 1960-62	61	26.8	6.8	18.7	10.7	1.9	5.6

TABLE 4. (*Continued*)

	Dura-tion of Period (years) (1)	Rate of Growth per Decade(%)			Coefficient of Multiplication in a Century		
		Total product (2)	Popu-lation (3)	Prod-uct per capita (4)	Total product (5)	Popu-lation (6)	Prod-uct per capita (7)
United States							
15. 1839 to 1960-62	122	42.5	21.6	17.2	34.5	7.1	4.9
Canada							
16. 1870-74 to 1960-62	89	40.7	19.1	18.1	30.3	5.7	5.3
Japan							
17. 1879-81 to 1959-61	80	42.0	12.3	26.4	33.4	3.2	10.4
European Russia– U.S.S.R.							
18. 1860-1913	53	30.2	13.8	14.4	14.0	3.6	3.8
19. 1913-58	45	35.7	6.4	27.4			
20. 1928-58	30	53.8	6.9	43.9	74.1	1.9	38.0

NOTES

For terminal periods longer than one year, duration was calculated from the mid years; and population for the midyear was used.

Product figures are in constant prices and refer to gross national product, gross domestic product, national income, and for Denmark to total available supply (gross domestic product at market prices plus net imports of goods and services).

Extension of the records to the most recent years, that is, those beyond the latest year mentioned in the specific country notes below, was made by means of the latest product series, kindly supplied by the Statistical Office of the United Nations, and by the population series given in the United Nations, *Demographic Yearbook*, usually the 1962 issue.

In every case two of the rate series (usually total product and population) were derived directly, and the third (usually per capita product) was calculated from the relatives of the other two.

Lines 1-3: Underlying data are from Phyllis Deane and W. A. Cole, *British Economic Growth, 1688-1959*, Cambridge, England, 1962. For line 1 we used the total and per capita output, given in fn. 1, p. 78; for line 2 we used the 1780 and 1800 figures also given there and the figures for 1801 and 1881 given in Table 72, p. 282; for line 3 we used Table 90, pp. 329ff, deriving population by means of the current price data, and national income as the product of popula tion and per capita.

ne 4: Total product and population from 1841-50 to 1861-70 (including Alsace-Lorraine); from 1871-80 to 1901-10 (excluding Alsace-Lorraine); and from 1901-10 to 1913 (including Alsace-Lorraine) are given in Simon Kuznets, "Quantitative Aspects of the Economic Growth of Nations, I. Levels and Variability of Rates of Growth," *Economic Development and Cultural Change,* 5:59 (October 1956), Appendix Table 3; and from 1913 to 1950 are given in Ingvar Svennilson, *Growth and Stagnation in the European Economy* (Geneva, 1954), Table A-1, p. 233, for product and Table A.4, p. 236, for population.

nes 5 and 6: Total and per capita product for 1851-55 to 1913 are from W. G. Hoffmann and J. H. Müller, *Das Deutsche Volkseinkommen, 1851-1927* (Tübingen, 1959), Table 2, p. 14, and Table 14, pp. 39-40 (1913 boundaries); for 1913 to 1935-37 (1925 boundaries) and for 1936 to 1950-52 (West Germany) are from Paul Jostock, "The Long-Term Growth of National Income in Germany," in Simon Kuznets, ed., *Income and Wealth, Series V* (London, 1955), Table I, p. 82.

ne 7: Total and per capita income, 1900-04 to 1950-52, are from Netherlands Central Bureau of Statistics, *Statistische en econometrische onderzoekingen,* 2nd qu., 1955, entitled *Nationale Rekeningen, 1954,* Table 18, p. 93.

ine 8: Total product and population for 1880 to 1913 are given in, or derived from, Colin Clark, *Conditions of Economic Progress,* 3rd ed. (London, 1957), Table XI, p. 102. Total product for 1913 is interpolated between 1910 and 1930 by product of industry and transportation, given annually, as is total product for 1910, 1930, and 1948, in Claude Carbonnelle, "Recherches sur l'evolution de la production en Belgique de 1900 à 1957," *Cahiers Economiques de Bruxelles,* April 1959, p. 358. Total population for 1913 and 1920 is from Henri Bunlé, *Le Mouvement naturel de la population dans le monde, de 1906 à 1936* (Paris, 1954), Table 1, p. 170.

ine 9: Total product and population for 1890-99 and 1938 are from Clark, Table XXXVIII, p. 189, product given and population derived. Product for 1938 and 1954 is from United Nations, *Statistical Papers,* Ser. H, No. 9 (New York, 1956), Table 2, p. 10.

ine 10: Total available supply for 1870-74 to 1950-52 and total population for 1872 are from Kjeld Bjerke and Niels Ussing, *Danmarks Nationalprodukt, 1870-1950* (Copenhagen, 1958), Table 3, pp. 146-47 and Table 1, p. 142. Total population for 1920, comparable with 1872 is from Bunlé, Table 1, p. 171.

ine 11: Total product for 1865-74 to 1956 and population for 1870 are from Juul Bjerke, "Some Aspects of Long-Term Economic Growth of Norway since 1865" (mimeo.), a paper presented at the 1959 Conference of the International Association for Research in Income and Wealth, Table II.1, p. 12, Table IV.2, p. 28, and Table IV.3, p. 32.

ine 12: Total product for 1861-65 to 1950-52 is from Osten Johansson, "Economic Structure and Growth in Sweden, 1861-1953" (mimeo.), a paper presented at the 1959 Conference of the International Association for Research in Income and Wealth, Table 18, pp. 62-65. Total population in 1863 is from Eric Lindahl, Einar Dahlgren, and Karin Kock, *National Income of Sweden, 1861-1930* (London, 1937), Part Two, Table 64, pp. 4-5.

Lines 13 and 14: Total product and population for 1861-65 to 1950-52 are from Istituto Centrale di Statistica, *Indagine Statistica Sullo Sviluppo del Reddit Nazionale dell Italia dal 1861 al 1956, Annali di Statistica,* Ser. VIII, vol. (Rome, 1957), Table 37, pp. 251-52.

Line 15: Total output and population for 1839 to 1879 are from Robert E. Gallman "Commodity Output, 1839-1899," *Trends in the American Economy in the Nine teenth Century,* Studies in Income and Wealth, vol. 24 (National Bureau of Economic Research, 1960), Table 1, p. 16; for 1877-81 to 1929-33 from annu data underlying estimates in Simon Kuznets, *Capital in the American Econom* (National Bureau of Economic Research, 1961), Table R-26 (Variant III pp. 563-64 and Table R-37, pp. 624-26; for 1929-33 to 1960-62 from th *Economic Report of the President, January 1964* (Washington, D.C., 1964 Table C-3, p. 210 and Table C-16, p. 227. The 1960-62 estimates were adjuste to exclude Alaska and Hawaii.

Line 16: Total product for 1870-74 to 1950 and population for 1872 to 1920 ar from O. J. Firestone, *Canada's Economic Development, 1867-1953* (Londo) 1958), Table 83, pp. 240-41 and Table 87, p. 276 (product slightly revise for 1950 in Dominion Bureau of Statistics, *National Accounts, Income and Ex penditures, 1926-1950,* Ottawa, 1952).

Line 17: Total product and population are from unpublished revisions by Henr Rosovsky and Kazushi Ohkawa of estimates in Kazushi Ohkawa and others, *Th Growth Rate of the Japanese Economy Since 1878,* Tokyo, 1957.

Lines 18-20: For European Russia total product is from Raymond W. Goldsmith "The Economic Growth of Tsarist Russia, 1860-1913," *Economic Developmen and Cultural Change,* 9: 471 (April 1961). Population for the pre-Worl War I period and through 1928 is from Frank Lorimer, *The Population of th Soviet Union* (Geneva, 1946), Table A-2, p. 208 (for 1859 and 1897, Europea Russia only); Table 15, p. 35 (for 1897 and 1914, prewar European Russia) Table 16, p. 36 and Table 54, p. 135 (for 1914 and 1928, post-World War Soviet area). We assumed that per capita income in 1928 was the same as i 1913, an assumption supported by the Birmingham Bureau of Research o Russian Economic Conditions, *Memorandum Number 3,* The National Incom of the U.S.S.R., November 1931, the table on p. 3.

For 1928-58 the estimates are from Simon Kuznets, "A Comparative Ap praisal," in Abram Bergson and Simon Kuznets, eds., *Economic Trends in th Soviet Union* (Cambridge, 1963), Table VIII.2, p. 337.

| | Duration of Period (decades) (1) | Share of Agriculture in Labor Force (%) | | Change in Shares per Decade | | | Rate of Growth of Labor Force (% per decade) (7) |
| | | Initial date (2) | Terminal date (3) | Absolute A(—) or Non-A(+) (4) | Percentage of initial base | | |
					A (5)	Non-A (6)	
1. Great Britain, 1831-1951	12.0	25	5	1.7	—12.6	2.0	10
2. France, 1866-1951	8.5	43	20	2.7	— 8.6	4.1	2
3. Belgium, 1880-1947	6.7	24	11	1.9	—11.0	2.4	5
4. Switzerland, 1880-1941	6.1	33	20	2.1	— 7.9	3.0	8
5. Netherlands, 1899-1947	4.8	28	17	2.3	— 9.9	3.0	15
6. Denmark, 1870-1950	8.0	52	23	3.5	— 9.2	5.9	11
7. Norway, 1875-1950	7.5	49	25	3.2	— 8.6	5.3	11
8. Sweden, 1870-1950	8.0	55	19	4.5	—12.4	7.6	9
9. Italy, 1901-51	5.0	49	35	2.8	— 6.5	5.0	7
10. United States, 1840-1950	11.0	68	12	5.1	—14.6	9.6	24
11. Canada, 1901-51	5.0	44	19	5.0	—15.5	7.7	24
12. Japan, 1872-1950	7.8	76	33	5.5	—10.1	14.1	13
13. U.S.S.R., 1928-58	3.0	71	40	10.3	—17.4	27.4	22

NOTES

Agriculture in most countries includes forestry and fishing.

Columns 2 and 3: From Clark, Table III, pp. 510-20, except for Great Britain, Denmark, and the U.S.S.R. Great Britain (line 1) is from Deane and Cole, Table 30, p. 142; Denmark (line 6) is from Bjerke and Ussing, Table I, pp. 142-43;

U.S.S.R. (line 15) is from Kuznets, "A Comparative Appraisal," in *Econom* *Trends in the Soviet Union*, Table VIII.6, p. 344.

Column 4: Difference between columns 2 and 3 divided by column 1, negative f‹ the share of agriculture and positive for the share of nonagriculture.

Column 5: Proportional decline per decade from the initial to the terminal date.

Column 6: Proportional rise per decade from the initial to the terminal date, base‹ on the complements of columns 2 and 3.

Column 7: Derived from the sources cited in the notes to columns 2 and 3 with th following exceptions: for Sweden the labor force figures are from Clark, Tab‹ XXXVII, pp. 181-85; for Great Britain from Deane and Cole, Table 31, p. 14: for the U.S.S.R. from Abram Bergson, "National Income," in *Economic Tren‹* *in the Soviet Union*, Table I.1, p. 4.

Lecture III

THE AFTERMATH
OF WORLD WAR II

THE DESIGNATION of the multinational conflicts of 1939-45 and 1914-18 as *world* wars is semantic liberty—for not all of the world was engaged in either. Practically all of Latin America avoided effective participation; much of colonial Asia and Africa was far less deeply involved than the metropolitan powers; and even the engagement of some avowed legal participants—Japan and Portugal in World War I or Brazil in both world wars—was quite limited. These differences in intensity of participation, in the degree to which the actively engaged nation-states suffered invasion and the destructive effect of battles fought in their territories, and in the outcome of the war for them, meant, naturally, different impacts of war on their economies, with consequently different prospects for postwar economic growth. In this light, neither of the two world wars was universal. But it would be extremely awkward to designate these conflicts by the names of participants, even if we limited them to the six to ten major active ones (the full list for 1939-45 includes 28 countries); and it is true that the economic and political magnitudes of the countries involved were such that the conflicts dominated the world scene. It is thus useful to retain the appellation, to distinguish these wars from others far more limited in the numbers and magnitudes affected.

We are concerned here with the aspects of World War II that seem to have most bearing on the interpretation of post-World War II economic growth. There are two difficulties. The selection assumes that we know which aspects of the war had the greatest effect on the patterns of the postwar economic growth; and our knowledge is limited. Then, after having made our selection, we must specify the impact, the aftermath; and that is difficult, partly because the data are not at hand, partly because adequate measures have not yet been formulated. This last statement suggests that it may be almost impossible to assign weights to war experience and its impact in terms comparable to those of peacetime economic activity—to translate somehow the horrors of war into dollars and cents; and the very attempt to do so may seem inappropriate, since it is bound to disregard the very essence of the effect of war on human beings and societies. All this is acknowledged; and yet mankind lives on after a war and carries on its peaceful (and war-oriented) pursuits, and this activity is affected in tangible ways by the aftermath of the war. These effects must be taken into account if we are to understand postwar experience; they cannot be ignored on the grounds that the war is in a realm separated from times of peace by an unbridgeable gulf.

Three aspects of World War II will be touched upon here: the magnitude of the economic losses involved; the effects connected with changes in technology, in institutions, and in the scales of priorities; and the associated shifts in political diversity and world structure.

2

Theoretically, the economically relevant costs of the war could be estimated directly by calculating several items for all participating nations. For population, the calculation would cover the number of combatants (and noncombatants) killed

and maimed; the excess deaths due to diseases associated with
the war; and the loss resulting from reduced marriage and
birth rates. All this would have to be studied in its differential
impact on age and sex groups, and on the structure of the
population at the end of the war. For material capital the
calculation would aim to establish the value of capital within
the country destroyed as a result of the war activities, but
excluding the excess depreciation reflected in war expenditures. The latter are the next items to be calculated in terms
of real resources, net of war production facilities that may
have some peace-type uses after the war (or uses for the
limited war production that may still be needed) and net of
any remaining and possibly still useful stocks of military
material. The sum of each of these three items—population,
material capital, and wasteful use of current output—for all
war participants (without cancellation) would represent the
total human and economic input into the war. For the years
directly following the conclusion of hostilities, further costs
may have been incurred either because of continuation of
conditions leading to further drains on potential population
growth or to lower than "normal" peacetime production levels
—which could be added for all nations affected; or because
of forced transfers of population, capital reparations, or
commitments of future output to uses of no benefit to the
losers—which when added for all nations involved would
cancel out, except for the sizable transfer and dislocation
costs.

Such direct estimates of war costs in terms of population
losses and losses of capital and output are beset with difficulties, and cannot easily be made with the data at hand. A
rough notion of the impact of the war can be derived, however, by comparing population and aggregate output (or,
better, output minus war production, where the latter is still
important) at the end of the war with prewar levels. Any

absolute decrease of population or output, or an increase over the period that is much lower than an estimate based on past patterns of growth in peaceful times, would suggest the magnitude of the war impact. Such a comparison necessarily assumes that the prewar year reflects a relatively normal position on the secular trend line, and that the postwar year reflects the full cumulative impact, before any recovery begins. Moreover, it tells us nothing of the movements *within* the period covered, and hence fails to indicate whether the levels for the terminal year prevailed only during that year or were in effect for several years. Yet it does indicate the levels at the end of the war, just before recovery begins; and does provide a partial summary of the possible effect of the war on recovery and the postwar growth that follows.

Table 6 provides such a summary, not only for the major countries that participated in World War II, but also for other countries for which the relevant national product data are available. The movements of national product, total and per capita, in several countries that participated in the war, suggest that 1945 is the most suitable common year for dating the full impact of the war—just before recovery began. We therefore used this date whenever data were available; and in all other cases a year close to it. The prewar base year was in most cases 1937, 1938, or 1939, depending upon availability of data, and the year with the highest product per capita when a choice was possible.

In order to approximate the degree of recovery attained immediately after the end of the war we also included the next five years, from 1945 to 1950. The choice of 1950 does not imply that the recovery was completed by that time, but it seemed useful to select one date fairly close to the end of the war for all countries, so that we could observe the extent of recovery and so provide a basis for consideration of the postwar growth after the immediate recovery phase.

Although Table 6 covers little of Africa and omits many countries in Asia, the coverage is wide enough, when supplemented by more global data on population, to give a rough idea of the quantitative impact of the war on population and per capita product.

(a) With few exceptions, of which the U.S.S.R., with its 10 percent drop in population between 1940 and 1944, was the most notable, the numbers even in the most actively participating and invaded (invaded meaning serving as theater of war) countries were somewhat greater at the end of the war than in the prewar years.[1] But these increases were clearly below the long-term "normal" level; and even by 1950 the population growth of many of the participating countries had not recovered completely, reflecting the large actual losses during the war compounded by appreciable losses in the demographic growth potential.

This finding is supported by decade data for the total population for major regions of the world.[2] A comparison of the rates of population growth per year in three periods, 1920-40, 1940-50, and 1950-60, reveals that in five of the fourteen large regions of the world, the rate of growth during the war decade, 1940-50, was significantly lower than that for 1920-40 and even more so than that for 1950-60. These five include the three regions of Europe (Northern and Western, Central, Southern and Eastern); the U.S.S.R., which, as already noted, shows an absolute decline over the decade; and the Southeast region of Asia, dominated by Indonesia, Burma, the Philippines, and Vietnam (which together accounted for some 80 percent of the region's total population in 1950). Certainly the first four regions listed were much affected by World War II, and in Southeast Asia turmoil continued well

---

[1] The unusually high level for West Germany reflects the large influx of refugees from East Germany and other areas.

[2] See United Nations, *Demographic Yearbook, 1961,* Table 2, p. 120.

beyond the end of the war in 1945. The combined rate of growth of these five regions was about 1.0 percent per year, or 10.4 percent per decade, for 1920-40; declined to 0.31 percent per year, or 3.2 percent per decade, for 1940-50; and then rose again to 1.31 percent per year in 1950-60. If there had been no war, with its immediate aftermath, and if the population in these five regions had grown in 1940-50 at the 1920-40 rates (which, for Europe, reflected a decade of economic depression and consequently depressed birth rates), total population for these regions would have grown from 728 million in 1940, not to the 751 million shown for 1950, but to about 806 million, or some 55 million more—about 15 million in Europe, about 31 million in the U.S.S.R., and about 9 million in Southeast Asia.[3] And this calculation does not allow for additional losses, of living population or of that still to be born, in the rest of Asia, particularly Japan and China, in North America, and in Oceania.

Rough as these calculations are, they do indicate that the war-induced losses, for already living population or that still to be born, run into tens of millions. This finding is hardly surprising. The areas affected by World War II cover most of the world, excluding Africa and Latin America, and accounted in 1940 for 1,942 million of the world total of 2,249 million. A 10 percent rise in this total over a decade is 194

---

[3] The figure for the U.S.S.R. is confirmed by a calculation by James W. Brackett in *Dimensions of Soviet Economic Power*. He estimates that population in the present territory at the time of the German attack in June 1941 was 200 million. With the 1959 census showing only 208.8 million persons, Mr. Brackett estimates that population "must have dropped to a low of somewhere between 170 and 175 million in 1945 or 1946. Thus, between 1941 and 1946 the Soviet Union experienced an absolute population decline of between 25 and 30 million" (p. 509).

He then goes on to examine the imbalance between males and females at the beginning of 1950, compared with the ratios in mid-1941, and suggests "that male military losses may have approached 15 million. This figure is markedly higher than previous estimates, the highest of which is about 9.5 million" (p. 510).

million, and a reduction of the rise by two to three percentage points represents a loss of some 39 to 58 million.

Three aspects of this population loss should be noted. First, the impact on the aggregate, including both actual and potential, was different for different major regions of the world. Europe and the U.S.S.R. were most severely affected; and even if we add Oceania and the Western Hemisphere to form a total that might be referred to as the population in the area of European settlement, the rate of growth of population for this area declines from 1.0 percent per year in 1920-40 to 0.64 percent per year in 1940-50; whereas the rate of growth for the rest of the world—Asia and Africa—rises from 1.14 percent per year in 1920-40 to 1.38 percent per year in 1940-50 —with the differential, unfavorable to the area of European settlement, increasing from 0.14 percent to 0.74 percent per year. (It amounted to 0.49 percent per year in 1950-60).

Second, losses due to excess mortality are far larger than those due to a lower birth rate, and they represent a far greater loss of human capital, of people trained in different skills and equipped with a variety of valuable experiences. Recent estimates set the casualties of Germany (combatants and civilian population killed in bombing) at 4.2 million; the armed casualties of the European allies of Germany (Austria, Italy, Rumania, Hungary) at close to 1.5 million; of Japan at 1.5 million; of France, the United Kingdom, and the United States at close to 1 million.[4] With 10 to 15 million military casualties for the Soviet Union, the excess deaths of civilian population not included above, the deaths resulting from the genocide policies of Germany against Jews and other racial

---

[4] See B. Ts. Urlanis, *Wars and the Population of Europe* (in Russian), Moscow, 1960, pp. 193-250. Curiously, Mr. Urlanis does not give precise figures of casualties for the U.S.S.R., although he provides specific estimates for other countries. But he does suggest that the losses in the U.S.S.R. were large by citing the imbalance after the war in the proportions of males and females in specific adult age groups.

groups, the total would come to 30 million or more. Although detailed and precise figures are not at hand, it is clear that large losses were sustained. In these days of concern over the present high rate of population growth, it may seem that such losses can easily be made up in the years that follow. But although this is true of numbers, it is not true either of the losses of able and trained people, or of the impact that these losses had on the survivors—the third comment relevant here.

The impact of these losses on specific countries has been radically different. It was particularly heavy in the invaded countries, but of moderate proportions in countries that, although actively engaged, were spared actual warfare on their territory. But whether proportionately heavy or light, the effects of direct contact with war by large proportions of the population in the participating countries, and particularly those invaded, must have gone far beyond the loss of numbers. This contact must have affected the shifts in the scales of values that contributed, as will be suggested below, to the postwar developments.

(b) The relatives of per capita product in Table 6 (column 3) tell a somewhat more complicated story, and the findings can best be summarized if we distinguished several groups of countries.

The first group, exemplified by Germany, the U.S.S.R., and Japan, were active participants that were invaded; and their per capita products (at the end of the war) were at strikingly low relative levels. The relative levels of 48 percent for Netherlands, 57 percent for France, 47 percent for Italy, probably about that for West Germany in 1945 (it was 78 in 1948), 46 percent for Japan, and 30 percent for Greece clearly indicate that economic performance per head was appallingly low.[5] Although recovery in most of these countries in the

---

[5] While the estimates in Table 6 show for the U.S.S.R. a decline in total gross national product of only 18 percent by 1944, other evidence suggests much greater declines by 1945. Thus, the official index of gross

period immediately following and the relative rise in per capita product were quite rapid, per capita product in 1950 in several was still either below the prewar level, or close to it—reflecting an increase over a period longer than a decade that was far below the usual. In this connection the particularly slow recovery in some Asian countries—Burma, Indonesia, Taiwan, China, and even Japan—by 1950 is to be noted.

The second group includes countries that participated in the war but were not invaded and could maintain high levels of *total* output, aggregate and per head (the United Kingdom, United States, Canada, Union of South Africa, Australia). But active participation in the war meant the allocation of a large part of total output to war production, and a corresponding reduction in the share going to household consumption or peacetime uses in general (that is, total including peacetime capital formation and civilian government expenditures). Hence in the United States, Canada, Australia, and the Union of South Africa, per capita output net of government expenditure, was either lower or only moderately higher in 1945 than in the prewar base year. The implication for the economic growth processes after the end of the war is obvious.

The third group includes countries that were not active participants, but were so closely connected with participants that the conflict created disturbed conditions difficult to adjust to. Thus it is curious, but perhaps not puzzling, that the per capita product in Switzerland in 1945 was below its prewar base; that per capita product in Sweden grew much less between 1939 and 1945 than between 1945 and 1950; that per capita product in New Zealand dropped slightly between 1937 and 1945 but rose sharply between 1945 and 1950; that

---

agricultural output declined 40 percent from 1940 to 1945 (see D. Gale Johnson, "Agricultural Production," in *Economic Trends in the Soviet Union*, Table V.3, p. 208). Value added in production of manufactured civilian goods, in 1950 prices, declined more than 50 percent from 1940 to 1945 (see Raymond P. Powell, "Industrial Production," in *ibid.*, Table IV.2, p. 160).

the movements were similar in Argentina, Brazil, and Southern Rhodesia, where per capita product was lower in 1945 than in 1939.

The fourth group comprises countries for which the war period offered unusually favorable opportunities for growth because, by remaining neutral, they did not suffer any interruption of peacetime trade relations and profited from the war-induced increased markets for their products. But the only country in Table 6 in which the rise in per capita product suggests these conditions is Mexico; and perhaps because it is so close to the United States, whose total output and demand expanded greatly, and it did not need to concentrate on war production, Mexico does belong to this group. There may have been other countries in Latin America or Africa in a similar position, but the available data do not cover them.

While the effect of decline and incomplete recovery in per capita product suggested in Table 6 will be discussed more explicitly in connection with postwar growth in the last lecture, two findings may be noted here. First, in many developed countries the rate of change from the prewar year to 1950 was much below the rate of growth in per capita product in the past. If the latter is set roughly at between 15 and 20 percent per decade, many of the *developed* countries in Europe covered in Table 6 fell distinctly short of this growth level. Second, the countries of Asia, by and large, show only moderate rises in per capita product by 1950, compared with prewar years. Indeed, per capita product in the major populous countries at the end of the war decade is quite low, and shows little gain over the prewar levels.

3

For population and output we could measure actual losses, or, by comparing the normal rates of growth with those that occurred during the war period, derive an approximate measure of total impact. When we turn now to such important determinants of economic growth as technology, social institutions, and the scale of value priorities of human beings, we have no quantitative gauges and the task of evaluating the impact of a major war becomes complicated indeed. While no firm answers can be given or expected, a considered formulation of the questions may be of some help in orienting our thinking.

It was stressed in our earlier discussion that the increasing stock of technological knowledge is a major determinant of modern economic growth: it makes possible, given the proper adjustment of economic and social institutions, the high rate of aggregate growth and rapid structural shifts that ensue. A major war affects technological change by concentrating resources on types of technological innovation that are of particular value to the military conflict, and by directing resources away from technological innovation in peace-type production. The mobilization of highly skilled and related resources away from basic research and concern with peace-type product (often market-oriented), on the one hand, and toward technological innovations with immediate application in the war effort, on the other, is particularly important in the developed countries, for it is these countries that have large volumes of such resources. Hence mobilization and redirection of these resources can have a large impact on the rate and direction of technological change. Thus the result of such an effort during World War II has been an impressive list of war-induced technological innovations, ranging from the use of atomic fission for the production of energy, to radar, to new communication devices, to missiles and satellites. Undoubtedly, too, a vast variety of less conspicuous technological innovations in production practices and devices originated in connection with new products and production problems generated by the war. It is beyond my competence to compile such a list, but we may assume that it is impressive.

Given such a list, we are faced with two important questions; and because they are typical of other nonmeasurable determinants of economic growth, we formulate them explicitly. First, what is the economic magnitude of the war-induced technological innovations? What opportunities do they provide for economic growth, such growth being defined in terms of the desired economic output per worker or per capita? The answer to this question would measure the *gross* prospective contribution of war-induced technological innovations to the defined goals implicit in economic growth—obviously no easy task. To be sure, one may claim, for example, that the practical production of atomic energy is an innovation that must eventually have wide repercussions, not unlike those associated with the introduction and spread of steam power, electric power, and the internal combustion engine. In that sense, the gross magnitude of this war-induced innovation is enormous; but the time and spatial pattern of its spread are quite uncertain. And this qualification applies to all attempts to measure the contribution to growth of any major technological innovation, particularly if reference is made to a base for economic growth over a relatively limited period, either directly after the war or following some immediate recovery phase.

Second, what is the economic magnitude of innovations foregone because of the war effort, which constitute the opportunity cost of the innovations actually originated? Obviously, we cannot measure what might have happened; but we could attempt to proceed as we did with the growth of population and output and use the prewar rate of technological innovation as a standard. If there were such a standard, by comparing it with the rate of peace-type and war-induced technological innovations during the war period, we could derive the *net* impact of war diversion of resources. But what magnitudes and time patterns shall we assign to technological innovations in the prewar past? All that we usually measure is the post-facto growth of output per unit of input; and, to the best of my knowledge, there is no tested theory that traces the path from basic science to the emergence of technological innovations, to their gradual spread through the production system. We have no tested pattern of the origin, rate of growth, or spread of innovations that could be applied either to innovations foregone or to the war-induced innovations. Thus, to illustrate, if during the war years, and perhaps even later, much basic research has been foregone because of the diversion of creative resources to other uses, we cannot tell when the impact will be felt in future growth; or how great it will be.

These difficulties in the way of assigning weights to technological innovations—in their bearing upon potential economic growth for which they provide a base—and specifying the time pattern of effect, apply equally to war-induced changes in social and economic institutions, and in the beliefs, values, and patterns of behavior of individual members of societies. In the participating countries, particularly those not under authoritarian rule in peacetime, the war effort required a marked intensification of centralized controls; curbs on individual freedom, even if such curbs reflected general consensus; and a host of new devices—conscription, rationing, price controls, material controls, programming and planning—previously nonexistent. And even in the authoritarian countries, participation in the war meant intensification of controls. Granted that in the victorious democratic countries many war-originated social and economic institutions were eliminated shortly after the war, some (for example, compulsory military service, rent controls) remained for a number of years; and the others, although liquidated, are an integral part of experience, representing experiments that proved useful under specific circumstances and that could be revived, wholly or in part, under closely or even remotely similar conditions. In those authoritarian states like Germany, Italy, and Japan, where the institutions that led to the conflict were destroyed by its outcome, and the adjustment to the loss of the war necessitated a revolutionary and forced change, many internal political, social, and economic institutions were reshaped to patterns quite different from those that had prevailed for many years before the war. We need hardly argue further that in the participating countries the war produced marked changes in social and economic institutions, many of which survived to affect markedly the postwar years. Yet one would be hard put to it to assign magnitudes to these changes, and to compare them with the rate of institutional change that might be termed "normal" in the course of modern economic growth.

The war-induced changes in the beliefs and attitudes of man, in their bearing upon economic organization and policy and thus upon economic growth, must also have been large and widespread, and here we have even less tangible evidence than for technological and institutional innovations. The eruption of two sanguinary conflicts in the span of a single generation would surely shift emphasis more toward goals of security than toward those of market-oriented economic attainment. The example, during the war and even in some prewar years, of forceful departures by some countries from established economic practices that were nevertheless successful in terms of augmented output and increased economic and related power made for an attitude that was more receptive to a variety of consciously designed economic rules and practices and more detached from beliefs generated by past economic practices and philosophy. If the Great Depression produced the Keynesian revolution in the accepted body of economic doctrine, the experience of the war and the immediate prewar years must have shaken even more the established economic views and philosophies, for it raised major questions about the relation of economic to other variables for the long-term destinies of economic societies—questions that might have been raised earlier if attention had not been concentrated on short-term problems in individual countries. Most important, people generally, and the responsible groups in societies faced with the war and its immediate antecedents and consequences, began to realize the long-term dependence of the society not so much on the market-tested economic performance but on the capacity to generate technological and social change as a basis for maintaining unity and security in a divided world; and had to recognize that unrestrained economic competition which had under peaceful conditions been legitimate and effective and promised an individual success on the basis of slowly operating market-approved tests, made less sense when the individual could be cut off in the prime of life by war and war-induced dangers. The strengthening of the welfare state in the non-Communist economies clearly reflected the changed views on the feasibility of unrelieved economic competition in a divided and insecure world; and, not surprisingly, the relaxation of the dictatorial control of the body of consuming and creative groups in the U.S.S.R., the one major authoritarian state that survived active participation in the war, was also due to the realization that the millenial pie-in-the-sky does not suffice if the physical security of the present—and even of the next—generation, is threatened. These may be only some of the shifts in attitudes and beliefs on the relation between man and social order that have occurred because of, or been intensified by, the war. But we have no way of gauging their potential effects on economic growth.

Although we cannot measure the net contribution to subsequent economic growth of war-induced changes in technology, institutions, and beliefs and attitudes we can speculate on the basis of crude impressions. Such speculation involves evaluating the impact of all these changes on some kind of economic growth—and we use here the type of economic growth that occurred in the postwar years, not some other type that could be envisaged in the light of other notions governing economic attainment. This base of reference predetermines to some extent the conclusion that is suggested, for the war-induced changes themselves made the kind of economic growth that occurred more likely than other types.

It would appear that the balance of war-induced technological innovations, of changes in social and economic institutions, and of shifts in man's attitudes, particularly in the participating developed countries and other developed countries that could profit, provided a base for greater economic growth, at least in the relatively short period following the immediate postwar recovery, than might otherwise have been expected. This impression is based on the magnitude and variety of the technological innovations; on the greater tendency toward a deliberate shaping of social and economic institutions in order to enhance economic growth—a goal that became, in many countries, a more clearly accepted responsibility of government than it was before; and on the changed climate of social opinion which placed greater emphasis not only on immediate opportunities rather than on those in the far future, but also on shortening and easing the competitive struggle under conditions of initial inequality—whether the latter was associated with age or parental economic position. The impact was different in the less developed countries. For many of these it meant attaining political independence and confronting many new problems which, in many cases, affected economic growth adversely—a point to which we shall return in the last lecture.

Three aspects of this tentative conclusion may be noted. First, it is limited to economic growth over the rather short period that has elapsed since the war or since the immediate postwar recovery years. It is difficult but not impossible to entertain a conception of the longer range of consequences that stretch several decades ahead. But it would require the construction of a chain of connections into the future on the basis of a number of links, each subject to a margin of error, so that the cumulative sum would make the ultimate consequence so chancy as hardly to merit explicit consideration.

Second, it can be argued that the war-induced changes would have emerged in the course of time even if there had been no war; that the technological innovations for which science has been ripe would have come; that the institutional changes designed to supplement the deficiencies of a market economy or reduce the limitations of a dictatorial authoritarian regime would have occurred; and that the changes in attitudes toward greater responsibility of society for overcoming initial inequalities would also have occurred—as continuations of underlying trends, all in good time. From this viewpoint, the war accelerated trends but did not create them; and accelerated them at a heavy cost. But this does not change our conclusion, for time is the axis against which we measure growth; and if war hastened some results, the accelerated rate of attainment is precisely what we mean when we say that war provided the basis for greater growth, unless it would be argued that such acceleration is to be followed inevitably by a compensating retardation.

The third and last comment is far more qualifying, and it is that our impression depends heavily upon accepting the kind of economic growth that took place in the last decade to a decade and a half. If we were to adopt different criteria of economic growth, for a presumably less divided world, the suggestion that the war-induced technological and social innovations made a positive contribution might not be tenable. The proper judgment in that case would depend upon the features of recent economic growth, with respect to composition of output, limitations on individual freedom, and emphasis on less desirable goals, that would be selected in reference to this different, and qualitatively preferable, type of economic growth.

4

World War II, like World War I, resulted in many major changes in the political organization of many parts of the world. It is not the intention here, nor am I competent, to survey these fully. But three shifts deserve brief mention because of their possible bearing upon rates of postwar economic growth.

(a) The first is the suppression of militarily oriented aggressive fascism in major countries like Germany, Italy, and Japan. We may, or may not, interpret World War II as stemming from the claims of these countries to greater political power over others, and from the incompatibility of the regimes so structured and oriented with the accepted mode of life of much of the rest of the world. It is the result that matters: the outcome of the war and the decision that such regimes could not be tolerated—with consequent changes in the political structure of these three major countries and of those of their satellites that were committed to this type of operation.

Both the defeat and the resulting institutional and political changes may have exercised major influence on postwar economic growth in these countries—not only in the recovery period when the huge material losses were made up, but probably even in the decade that followed. Germany, Japan, and, to a lesser extent, Italy, were and are among the more economically developed countries of the world. The collapse of the military- and power-oriented Fascist regimes and all the excesses committed during and immediately before the war may well have had a shocking effect on the societies involved—inducing a strong reaction to irresponsible adventurous policies and the accompanying mythologies, and a concentration on the task of peaceful rebuilding, with a higher priority attached to economic attainment than in the immediate, and perhaps even longer-range, past. If one adds to this effect the legal limitations on input of resources into military uses, and the reluctance of these countries to engage in military production even after the limitations were lifted; the survival of a large group of skilled and educated persons; and the continuing pattern of economic behavior common to economically developed countries, one would expect the postwar period to witness high rates of growth in these countries—even in the years beyond those of immediate recovery. And the drive toward higher rates of growth would be augmented by the increment to the stock of knowledge made during the war by some of the developed countries, which, while participating, still escaped the devastation of war—a stock that could be borrowed, once the pressures of immediate recovery were eased.

(b) The second major political consequence of World War II was the survival and expansion of the Communist pattern of organization. Originally limited to the U.S.S.R., it spread to much of Eastern Europe, primarily as a result of the pressures and claims of the Soviet Union; and more importantly it emerged in Mainland China, with outposts in North Korea and North Vietnam. Being essentially a minority regime bent upon rapid and radical changes in the society it attempts to dominate—changes that involve major sacrifices by the population—the Communist system, when not imposed from the outside, has so far managed to establish itself only when the political structure of a country has been weakened by great strain; and when the antecedent development has left a vacuum, in the sense that no effective social group evolved that could organize the society along more democratic and responsive lines. Despite continuous talk about class structure, the Communist regime is essentially the product of a classless group of professional politicians and revolutionary bureaucrats, operating by expeditious and changing appeals to different interests at different times without permanent commitment to any; and this detachment permits them to be ruthless in changing the existing structure of society.

It is thus hardly an accident that World War I, which imposed a great strain upon Russia, produced the first Communist country; that the prolonged war, which began in 1938, produced the Communist regime in Mainland China; and that both of these major countries were economically underdeveloped, with a social structure that was not conducive to the evolution of a strong economic group—from among the landlords, the masses of poor, unorganized peasants, and a small, underdeveloped urban proletariat—that could provide the basis for a more democratically oriented and effective political organization. Nor is it surprising—given the capacity of Communist rule to mobilize the energy to build up economic power, although at great sacrifice and with considerable waste, and the Hobson's choice offered by the Nazis to the Soviet people—that, after an initial debacle, resistance to Germany was finally organized, and with the help of the free developed countries, survival was assured.

Whatever the reasons for the survival and extension of the Communist pattern of organization, the effect on postwar economic growth was marked in several ways. The concentration of the old and the newly established Communist regimes on establishing the basis of economic power was bound to be reflected in high rates of growth, considering the implied composition of output and the emphasis on producers' goods which could be so much more effectively expanded through investments directed by a centralized autocratic state. Then, the divisive tendency introduced by the Communist regimes, with their vociferous hostility to the developed countries, created conditions that raised concern about economic attainment in those countries, as well as about security. Consequently, the major non-Communist developed countries that had not been significantly devastated by the war, particularly the United States, helped both their former allies and their former enemies rebuild as quickly as possible. This policy might in any case have been followed in the light of the disillusioning post-World War I experience with reparations and similar economic penalties, but it was clearly stimulated by the desire to contain the aggressive tendencies of the Communist countries. Finally, Communist drive was an additional incentive to extend assistance to the less developed countries, under the new and difficult conditions of their political independence—another program that might otherwise have come into being, but one that was clearly hastened by the threat of the Communist regimes and that, in fact, was later augmented by the Communist assistance program.

(c) The third major political consequence of World War II was the rapid shift of most colonial areas in Asia and Africa to independence from the developed non-Communist metropolitan countries. This dissolution of colonial bonds began soon after World War I with an emphasis on national self-determination and independence, the introduction of mandates and supervision, and a perceptible weakening of former ties between the metropolitan countries and their colonies. A number of factors conspired to speed the spread of political independence: the increasing realization of the limited gains from such ties, both to the colonies and to the metropolitan countries; the attempt during the war to enlist the cooperation of the colonies in a struggle that was not of their making, and the contradiction between the principles of freedom broadcast during the war by the victorious powers and the practice of dominion over colonies; the substantial weakening in the immediate postwar years of those metropolitan powers that participated in the war; and the growing disbelief in these developed countries in the long-term viability of the existing arrangements, given the expanding educated elites in the colonies and the paucity of benefits to the masses from colonial ties. In some cases this granting of political independence was a hasty shedding of responsibility by the metropolitan power; in others it was a fairly systematic process, although, even then, not without some violence and conflict; in still others, independence was achieved only after a prolonged armed struggle.

Having affected so many countries in so short a period, the process naturally yielded diverse results both with respect to the capacity to generate economic growth and to decisions regarding nonpolitical ties with the metropolitan country. The impact on economic growth in the newly established states over the last decade to decade and a half has been dependent on the duration and intensity of the struggle for independence; on the solutions of partition and minority problems, which may also have been accompanied by violence and forced migration (in India-Pakistan, for example); on the capacity of the native elites to manage the country; and, of course, on the shape and structure of the economic society surviving from the past. Obviously it is difficult to summarize these diverse conditions in a general statement; all I can reasonably suggest is that, in general, settled political conditions conducive to sustained economic growth could hardly have emerged within the short period that has elapsed since the process began in Asia, and the even shorter period for most of Africa.

Various other political consequences of World War II could be cited, particularly the intensification of nationalist feelings, on the one hand, and the tendency to form blocs, on the other, to offset the limitations of a small or even a large nation-state in a divided world. But the brief, and necessarily speculative comments above are probably sufficient—when added to the discussion concerning economic losses and war-induced changes in technology, social institutions, and prevailing beliefs—to provide the background for an explicit consideration of postwar economic growth.

| | Relatives of Levels in Year Indicated in Stub | | | | | |
| | 1945 | | | 1950 | | |
Country, Type of Product, and Prewar Year	Product (1)	Popu-lation (2)	Per capita prod-uct (3)	Product (4)	Popu-lation (5)	Per capita prod-uct (6)
EUROPE						
1. United Kingdom, national income, 1937						
a. Total	115	104	111	110	107	103
b. Excl. public authority expend.	72	104	70	105	107	98
2. Ireland, cons. expend., 1938	98	101	97	120	101	119
3. France, national income, 1937	54	95	57	110	101	108
4. Netherlands, national income, 1937	52	108	48	130	118	110
5. Denmark, total avail. supply, 1939	84	106	79	130	112	116
6. Norway, gross domestic product, 1939	103(1946)	106	97	132	110	119
7. Finland, net domestic product, 1938	86	102	84	122	109	112
8. West Germany, net domestic product, 1936	94(1948)	121	78	117	125	94
9. East Germany, gross national product, 1936				73	114	64
10. Italy, national income, 1939	49	104	47	107	108	99
11. Austria, gross national product, 1938	85(1948)	104	83	104	102	102
12. Greece, net domestic product, 1938	31	104	30	81	111	73
13. Switzerland, net national product, 1938	96	106	90	128	112	114
14. Sweden, gross domestic product, 1939	120	105	114	166	111	150

TABLE 6. (*Continued*)

| | Relatives of Levels in Year Indicated in Stub | | | | | |
| | 1945 | | | 1950 | | |
Country, Type of Product, and Prewar Year	Product (1)	Population (2)	Per capita product (3)	Product (4)	Population (5)	Per capita product (6)
15. Spain, national income, 1939	118	106	111	142	110	129
16. U.S.S.R., gross national product, 1940						
a. Total	82(1944)	90	91	120	92	130
b. Household cons.	62(1944)	90	69	111	92	120
17. Bulgaria, national income and net material product, 1939	80	111	72	117	115	102
18. Hungary, net material product, 1938	60(1946)	99	61	126	102	124
19. Rumania, net material product, 1938	67(1948)	102	66	100	105	95
UNITED STATES AND CANADA						
20. United States, gross national product, 1939						
a. Total	172	107	161	168	116	145
b. Excl. govt. expend.	105	107	99	161	116	139
21. Canada, gross national expend., 1939						
a. Total	164	107	154	180	119	152
b. Excl. govt. expend.	132	107	123	179	119	151
OCEANIA						
22. Australia, national income, 1938/39						
a. Total	121	107	113	175	120	146
b. Excl. govt. expend.	105	107	98	172	120	143
23. New Zealand, national income, 1937/38	105	106	99	153	120	128
LATIN AMERICA						
24. Mexico, gross domestic product, 1939	156	116	134	202	133	152
25. Argentina, gross national product, 1939	119	112	106	155	126	123
26. Brazil, national income, 1939	118	115	102	166	129	129

| | Relatives of Levels in Year Indicated in Stub | | | | | |
| | 1945 | | | 1950 | | |
Country, Type of Product, and Prewar Year	Product (1)	Popu- lation (2)	Per capita prod- uct (3)	Product (4)	Popu- lation (5)	Per capita prod- uct (6)
7. Chile, gross domestic product, 1940	122	109	111	140	120	117
8. Colombia, gross product, 1939	125	114	110	153	127	120
9. Latin America, gross domestic product, 1939	127	112	113	167	126	132
ASIA						
0. Japan, national income, 1939	49(1946)	108	46	84	118	72
1. Taiwan, net domestic product, 1938	55(1946)	110	50	105	135	78
2. Mainland China, gross domestic product, 1933						
a. 1933 prices				113[a]	114	99
b. 1952 prices				121[a]	114	106
3. Philippines, national income, 1938	96(1948)	122	79	109	128	85
4. Cambodia, gross domestic product, 1938				134[b]	129	104
5. India, national income, 1937/38-1939/40				110	117	94
6. Burma, gross domestic product, 1938	61(1947)	114	54	62	118	52
7. Indonesia, national income, 1938				96[b]	112	86
8. Turkey, net national product, 1938	121(1948)	119	101	124	124	100
AFRICA						
9. Union of South Africa, net national product, 1938						
a. Total	136	111	123	187	120	156
b. Excl. govt. expend.	124	111	112	189	120	158
0. Southern Rhodesia, national income, 1939	116	120	96	210	145	145

[a] 1952. [b] 1951.

NOTES

Product is in constant prices. Population, unless otherwise indicated, is from the *Demographic Yearbook, 1960.*

Relatives were calculated directly for two of the series and the relative for the third series was derived from these.

Dates in parentheses in column 1 apply also to columns 2 and 3; those in column 4 apply also to columns 5 and 6.

When a continuous series was available, the prewar year with the peak per capita product was used; and if no decline occurred, 1938 was used.

Line 1: Deane and Cole, Table 90, pp. 329-31, for product per capita and population. Product excluding public authority expenditures was derived by applying to total product the share of public authority expenditures, based on current price figures and given in *ibid.,* Table 91, pp. 332-34.

Lines 2, 11, 12, 17 (col. 4-6): United Nations, *Statistical Papers,* Ser. H, No. 4 (New York, 1953), Table 2, for total and per capita product. Line 17, col. 1-3 is based on *ibid.,* Ser. H, No. 1 (New York, 1952), Table 3.

Line 3: Svennilson, Table A.1, p. 233, for total product.

Line 4: Nationale Rekeningen, 1954, Table 18, p. 93, for total and per capita product.

Line 5: Bjerke-Ussing, Table III, pp. 146-47, for total product.

Line 6: National Accounts, 1900-1929, Table 14, pp. 128-29, for total product.

Lines 7, 8, 13, 25, 30, 31, 36, 38: U.N., *Statistical Papers,* Ser. H, No. 9 (New York, 1956), Table 2, for total and per capita product except West Germany (line 8), for which total product, given in Table 3, is used.

Line 9: Wolfgang F. Stolper, *The Structure of the East German Economy* (Cambridge, 1960), Table 163, p. 418 for total product and Table 2, p. 22, for population.

Line 10: Indagine . . . , Table 37, pp. 251-52, for total product and population.

Line 14: Johansson, Table 18, pp. 62-65, for total product.

Lines 15, 18, 26, 37, 40: U.N., *Statistical Papers,* Ser. H, No. 8 (New York, 1955), Table 2, for total and per capita product.

Line 16: Abram Bergson, *The Real National Income of Soviet Russia since 1928* (Harvard University Press, Cambridge, 1961), Table 51, p. 210, for total product, composite 1937 base, total for 1944 excluding Lend-Lease, and for total consumption; *ibid.,* Table K-1, p. 442, for population, postwar boundaries.

Line 19: Central Statistical Office, *Anuarul Statistic, 1963* (Bucharest, 1963), Table 38, p. 113, for total and per capita product.

Line 20: Economic Report of the President, January 1964, Table C-2, pp. 208-09, for total product and national defense; Table C-16, p. 227, for population.

Line 21: Bureau of Statistics, *National Accounts, Income and Expenditure, 1926-1950* (Ottawa, 1952), Table 3, pp. 28-29, for total product and government expenditures.

Line 22: Clark, Table IX, pp. 90-91, for total and per capita product. Exclusion of government expenditures by applying ratio to gross national expenditures in current prices (for underlying data see U.N., *Statistical Papers,* Ser. H, No. 3, New York, 1953, Table 5).

Line 23: Clark, Table XXX, pp. 171-72, for total and per capita product.

Line 24: E. P. Lopez, "El Producto National," in Fondo de Cultura Economica, *Mexico: Cinquanto Años de Revolucion,* I La Economia (Mexico, 1960), Table 2, pp. 587-89, for total product.

Line 27: U. N. Statistical Office records for total product.

Line 28: Alexander Ganz, "Problems and Uses of National Wealth Estimates in Latin America," *Studies in Income and Wealth, Vol. VIII,* Table III, p. 226, for total and per capita product.

Line 32: Liu and Yeh, Tables 8 and 9, pp. 94-95, for product and Table 24, p. 149, for population.

Line 33: U. N., *Statistical Papers,* Ser. H, No. 2 (New York, 1952), Table 3, for total and per capita product.

Line 34: U. N., *Economic Survey of Asia and the Far East, 1961,* Table 5, p. 170, for total product.

Line 35: K. Mukerji, "A Note on the Long-Term Growth of National Income in India, 1900/01 to 1952/53," a paper presented at the September 1960 Conference of the International Association for Research in Income and Wealth, held in Hong Kong, for product and population.

Lines 39 and 40: U. N., *Statistical Papers,* Ser. H, Nos. 3 and 5 (New York, 1953 and 1954), Table 2, for total and per capita product. The estimate for line 39b is derived by applying the percentage share of government to net geographical product in current prices (*ibid.,* No. 3, Table 3).

Lecture IV

POSTWAR ECONOMIC GROWTH: FINDINGS AND QUESTIONS

IN DISCUSSING postwar economic growth, we begin with a review of the available data on total product, population, and per capita product. The several questions that arise in evaluating postwar growth experience can best be discussed after we observe its actual dimensions.

Table 7 assembles estimates of rates of change in the 1950's, based usually on three-year averages of product centered on 1951 and 1961, and single-year values of population for 1951 and 1961. The underlying annual data for product thus extend from 1950 through 1962, and the use of averages at the terminal points is intended to reduce the transient or cyclical fluctuations—a device not needed for the more smoothly moving population series. The table covers almost all the developed non-Communist countries, twelve in Europe, the four overseas: the United States, Canada, Australia, and New Zealand, and the one in Asia—Japan; the major Communist countries: U.S.S.R., Mainland China, and seven in Eastern Europe; and a number of the less developed countries: Greece in Europe, the larger countries in Latin America and Asia, but none in Africa.

Aside from the general weakness of the estimates for the less developed countries, we face a particular problem with the official product estimates for the Communist countries. These relate to material product, thus excluding services not embodied in commodities; use price ratios that tend to favor the more rapidly growing sectors of producer goods; and the rates of growth shown by them are subject to larger upward biases than those for non-Communist countries. The checks and revisions made by Western scholars of the product estimates for the U.S.S.R. and Mainland China, yield rates of growth in product (shown in Table 7), much lower than those shown by the official estimates; and the revisions cannot be ignored. If rough comparability with measures for non-Communist countries is to be attained, we must accept the available revisions and apply a parallel adjustment to the estimates for those Communist countries that have not been revised. Thus for six Eastern European Communist countries we assumed that the proportional exaggeration in the growth rates during the 1950's was the same as for the U.S.S.R.; and we used similarly crude assumptions to derive comparable estimates for the longer period back to the late 1930's. For East Germany a careful independent estimate is available through 1958.

Despite the crudity of the estimates and the adjustments that had to be applied to some of them, the general finding for the decade of the 1950's is fairly clear. With significant exceptions, the rate of growth in total and per capita product was quite high—certainly for the developed non-Communist countries in comparison with the rates that prevailed in the long-term past; for the less developed countries, for which we have no such records but can reasonably assume low rates of growth in the long-term past; and also for the Communist countries.

This general finding can be supported by reference to Table 7. In the developed countries of Europe, total product grew in the 1950's at decadal rates ranging from 30 percent for the United Kingdom to 103 percent for Germany, with most rates within the range from 40 to 60 percent; while per capita product grew at rates ranging from 24 to 81 percent, with most rates within the range from 24 to somewhat over 40 percent. The long-term rates of growth of total product, as indicated in Table 4, ranged for the developed countries of Europe between 20 and 37 percent; and those of per capita product between 14 and 28 percent. In Japan the excess of the growth rates in the 1950's over those in the long-term past was even greater. The significant exceptions among the developed non-Communist countries were the United States and Canada: in both countries the rate of growth of per capita product in the 1950's was between 10 and 13 percent, while the long-term rate was well above 15 percent per decade.

The Communist countries also show substantial rates of growth in total and per capita product in the 1950's, even when revised downward. The rates of increase in per capita product, ranging from over 25 to over 60 percent per decade (excluding the exceptional case of East Germany), must be well above those that prevailed in these countries in the long-term past. This is certainly true of Mainland China and the Eastern European countries; and is directly indicated by comparison of the high rate for the 1950's for the U.S.S.R. (62.4) with that for the three decades from 1928 to 1958 shown in Table 4 (43.9).

Even in the less developed countries, the rates of growth of total and per capita product in the 1950's are quite high, but with some significant exceptions. The high rates are shown for Greece, several countries of Latin America (Brazil, Mexico, Colombia, Puerto Rico); and several countries in Asia (Burma, Taiwan, Indonesia, Philippines, Turkey, Thailand, with moderate but substantial rates for India and Cambodia). However, a few countries show rather low rates of growth in the 1950's (Argentina and Chile among the larger countries in Latin America; Pakistan and Ceylon in Asia). Omitting Africa

from the discussion because of lack of data, we may conclude
that for most of the underdeveloped countries in Latin America
and Asia, rates of growth in total and per capita product in
the 1950's were fairly high. In Latin America they may not
have been higher—and in some countries may even have been
lower—than those in the preceding decades (at least back to
1927); but they surely were well above the low long-term
growth rates in the populous countries of Asia.

These findings lead us to inquire into the extent to which
the growth rates in the 1950's were still affected by recovery
from the war—a relevant question since, as we saw in Table 6,
per capita product in 1950 in many countries was either
below the level of the late 1930's or not much above it. The
question, in other words, is whether the growth of per capita
product in the 1950's was still a matter of "catching up," in
the double sense of recovering the actual material losses
sustained during the war and of compensating for the failure,
during the war and immediate pre- and postwar years, to
exploit the technological and other advances made elsewhere
in the world. The relevance of this question is pointed up by
Table 7, which shows that among the developed non-Communist countries the highest rates of growth in per capita
product in the 1950's are for Japan, Germany, Austria, and
Italy—the countries that sustained the greatest material losses
during the war; while the lowest rates are for the United
States and Canada—countries that were able to continue their
technological and other advances even in wartime.

A tentative answer is provided by columns 4-6 of Table 7,
in which the rates of growth are extended to cover a period
back to a pre-World War II year—usually in the late 1930's
(between 1937 and 1940, with the exception of Germany for
which the prewar year is 1936 and China for which it is
1933). The rates are therefore for a period from a prewar year
close to the beginning of the war and the end of the 1950's,

usually the three-year average centered in 1961. If the rates of growth in the 1950's are unusually high because of the after-effects of the war, those for the longer period back to the late 1930's should be much lower; and may even be close to the long-term rate, assuming that the recovery process has been completed or has not been pushed beyond the prewar growth pattern.

These measures for the longer period suggest three interesting findings. First, for the developed non-Communist countries, the Communist countries, and Latin America, the rates of growth in total and per capita product are still substantial. Concentrating on per capita product, we find that the decadal rates range from 12 to 38 percent for the developed non-Communist countries, and thus have about the same range as the long-term rates in Table 4; from less than 6 to 45 percent for the Communist countries, the low exceptions being Mainland China in which, for obvious reasons, the rate back to 1933 is low, and East Germany; and averaging 25 percent for Latin America, not much different from the rates for the developed non-Communist countries.

But, second, for several less developed countries in Asia, despite substantial growth in the 1950's, the rate of growth in per capita income over the longer period back to the late 1930's is quite low. In Burma and Indonesia, per capita product actually declines from the prewar levels; in India, the Philippines, and probably Pakistan, the rate is 5 percent or lower; and in Taiwan it is less than 9 percent. It seems clear that for the large populations of Asia (including Mainland China), amounting in the countries just listed to 1.4 billion, or almost half of the world total, the rate of growth in per capita product since the 1930's, and probably since the 1920's, was quite low—most likely below 5 percent per decade. Yet these are the countries in which the per capita income levels were, and are, among the lowest.

Third, the shift from the 1950's to the longer period back to the late 1930's changes significantly the relative standing of the developed non-Communist countries with respect to the growth rates in per capita product. Japan, Germany, and Italy, with the highest rates in the 1950's, are no longer at the top of the list for the period since the late 1930's; and the United States and Canada, which showed the lowest rates for the 1950's, are close to the top in column 8. Thus, in several important cases, the high rates of growth in the 1950's may still be reflecting recovery from the consequences of the war; while in others the relatively low rates in the 1950's may be in the nature of reactions to unusually high rates in the preceding decade to decade and a half.

This finding for the developed countries raises a further question that may be dealt with briefly before we turn to the possible explanations and implications. The period since the late 1930's begins at the end of a major depression, which affected significantly most of the developed non-Communist countries—as well as a number of the less developed countries. Consequently the growth rates may be exaggerated for the period from the late 1930's to the end of the 1950's, since it begins with only partial recovery from the depression but ends in years that were free from such effects. To put it differently, the rates of growth for the 1950's (or some earlier years) may reflect increases that are in the nature of recovery not only from the war and its aftermath but from the effects of the depression that were not completely overcome even by the late 1930's. By extending the period still further back to the late 1920's, we can see how completely the growth after World War II "made up" for the effects of both the war and the depression—by comparing the rates for that period with those characteristic of the economy's growth for the long-term periods before the late 1920's.

Table 8 provides the relevant measures for the period from

1927 to 1960, and for purposes of comparison gives those for earlier periods back to 1880, for thirteen developed countries with long-term records; and it also gives measures for 1927-60 for the major countries of Latin America and for Latin America as a whole. The evidence for the thirteen developed countries, which is of most interest to us here, shows that only in Belgium and France were the rates of growth in per capita product during 1927-60 lower than those prevailing over the longer periods in the past—at about 11 to 12 percent per decade compared with close to 20, or above 20, percent back to 1880. In most countries, the rate of growth in per capita product for the period since 1927 is not too different from the average for the long period back to 1880—although it is in some instances higher or lower than the rate for one or the other of the two long past periods shown. This rough equality of the rate of growth in per capita product in the recent long period and in the earlier long periods, which can be observed by comparing the entries in columns 1 and 4, is found for Denmark, Netherlands, Switzerland, the United Kingdom, United States, Canada, and Japan. In Norway, Germany,[1] Italy, and Sweden, the rate of growth in per capita product since 1927 is above that prevailing since 1880.

Table 8 clearly indicates that both the depression and the war were sufficiently offset by the spurt of postwar growth, so that the rates of growth of per capita product for the full period since 1927, with the exception of those for Belgium and France, were not inferior to those for five to six decades before

---

[1] The comparison for Germany is affected by changes in boundaries. The comparison back to the mid-1930's is for the present territory; and is linked with changes within the old territory for earlier periods. The change is large, since the population of West Germany at the time of linkage (1936) was only about six-tenths of the total of the old state. It may well be that the past rate of growth within the present territory of the West German Republic was significantly higher than that of the old Reich as a whole, since it comprised the more industrialized regions.

1927. Indeed, for several countries, particularly Germany and Italy which suffered heavily during the war, the growth rate for the period since 1927 was distinctly higher than that for the earlier long-term periods—although the comparison for Germany is subject to qualifications cited in footnote 1; and the same was true for Norway, also significantly affected by the war, as well as Sweden.

2

An adequate evaluation of the postwar growth experience, summarized above, requires three further distinct but related tasks. The first is a critical examination of the underlying product estimates, not only those for the Communist countries for which no independent estimates have been prepared but, more importantly, for most underdeveloped countries in Asia, Africa, and Latin America. The basic primary data are woefully weak; and careful scrutiny of the components of the aggregate product totals might suggest revisions and judgments that could affect significantly the results not only for the 1950's but also for earlier periods. This task is beyond the powers of any one investigator and would require years of concentrated effort by both scholars and governments. We should therefore keep in mind the great weakness of the estimates for many Communist and underdeveloped countries. We use them here on the optimistic assumption that the broad conclusions they suggest have some validity, and can add to our knowledge without adding to our confusion.

The next task would be to examine the relation of the components of the product totals thus tested—in all countries— to establish at least the proximate determinants of the growth in the aggregate. The allocation of growth by industrial sectors; the movement of the shares of labor and capital inputs; the effect of accumulated needs and a less unequal distribution of income on demand; the contribution of foreign trade and other foreign flows; the various aspects of the growth-affecting policy of government—all these would have to be considered in relation to the rate of growth achieved. And this intensive analysis would have to be made country by country.

But, third, such an analysis of the immediate determinants of recent growth would have to be placed in proper historical perspective to yield tenable results. The relations, for the recent postwar period among the sectors, factors, and other components of the economy in their contribution to aggregate growth, would have to be viewed against the background of a long-term past in which the trends in such relations could be discerned. Only such a background would provide the basis for judging the characteristics of the processes in recent years, studying their possible dependence upon some specific aspects of the long-term past, and suggesting their possible contribution in the future. Thus the analysis would require an examination not only of the postwar period but of the longer period.

None of these ambitious tasks can be attempted here, even for the developed countries for most of which the necessary data for recent years are available; and for some of which monographic studies of growth covering a long period are also at hand.[2] Within the limits of the present lecture, we can deal only with the broad aggregates; raise some obvious, but not all the significant, questions; and answer them only in a speculative and illustrative fashion. We have selected four; and these relate to: (a) the high rates of growth in the 1950's in most of the developed non-Communist countries of Europe and in Japan; (b) the relatively low rates of growth in the United States and Canada in the same decade; (c) the rates

---

2 Such studies for several countries in Europe, the United States, and Japan, have recently been initiated under the auspices of the Committee on Economic Growth of the Social Science Research Council.

of growth in the Communist countries; and (d) the contrast between the rates for the developed and Communist countries, on the one hand, and those for the less developed countries, on the other.

(a) The evaluation of economic growth during a period as short as a decade is beset with difficulties—a point that applies to our findings for all countries, but particularly for the developed non-Communist countries. The major source of the difficulties is the sensitivity of economic activity to transient disturbances connected with business cycles in the developed non-Communist countries—which have their parallels in the crop and foreign market cycles in the underdeveloped countries, and in cumulations of planning errors and difficulties in the Communist countries; and there are other kinds of changes in economic activity—for example, in the case of the 1950's, the effects of a war, of political shifts, and the like. By growth we mean significant and sustained aggregative and structural changes over a long period—not those that fluctuate, increasing in one decade and declining in the next. If the period is long enough—and for the present purposes three decades to half a century is sufficient—the measures themselves indicate whether a change of significant dimensions has been sustained and irreversible; and the longer the period, the more specific our measures can be, for the growth component can then be distinguished more readily from the transient components. But in studying data for a decade, let alone a few years, we cannot easily separate the growth element—the sustained long-term change—from the transient one that will be gone, canceled by an expected reaction, in the immediate future. This comment suggests that the common practice, of which we all are guilty, of talking about a rise over a year or two in GNP as *growth*, is misleading—for without elaborate analysis, and possibly not even then, we have no assurance that a specific rise is a movement along a long-term growth line, or, in other words, that it does not contain a large transient element (a cyclical boom or some other favorable but temporary disturbance); or that, because of some transient depressing disturbance, the increase shown is less than actual growth.

Furthermore, over short periods the rate of growth of *per capita* product will vary more than that of total product, since many of the transient components affect the growth rates of total product more than those of population. If, for purposes of illustration, we assume that the rate of growth of population remains the same from one short period to the next, the proportionate change in the rate of growth of per capita product is bound to be wider than that in the rate of growth of total product—amplification being a positive function of the ratio of the rate of growth of population to that of total product. To illustrate: if we assume that the rate of growth of total product for a given decade is 30 percent, and that of population is 15 percent, the rate of growth of per capita product is 13.0 percent. If the rate of growth of total product rises a third during the next decade, becoming 40 percent, and the rate of growth of population remains the same, the rate of growth of per capita product rises to 21.7 percent, or two-thirds; and if the rate of growth of total product declines a third, becoming 20 percent, the rate of growth of per capita income drops to 4.3 percent, or about two-thirds. If, with the same rates and changes for total product, the rate of growth of population is assumed to be 20, rather than 15, percent, the one-third increase in the rate of growth of total product raises the rate of growth of per capita product from 8.3 to 16.7, or doubles it; and the decrease of a third in the growth rate of total product reduces the rate of growth of per capita product to zero. Thus, a high ratio of the growth rate of population to the growth rate of total product makes the growth rate of per capita product particularly sensitive to even minor proportional declines in the rate of growth of total product.[3]

In Tables 7 and 8 we supplemented the measures for the 1950's by rates for much longer periods. This is the general practice in testing the sustained or long-term character of changes, since measures for successive (*not* overlapping) periods of, say, two decades each, would show much less variation than those for successive single decades, and measures for successive periods of three decades would show less variation than those for periods of two decades, and so on—as long as the periods belong to the same epoch and are not separated by any revolutionary breaks. Hence, if the parameter for a two-decade period is larger or smaller than that for the preceding two decades, the difference is more significant than the one revealed by measures for two successive single decades; and the same holds for a set of three-decade, compared with a set of two-decade, periods.

The hypothesis underlying this statistical procedure was already suggested in our discussion of the rates of growth for the different periods in Tables 7 and 8. In application to the 1950's, the hypothesis implies that war damage—material losses (or disturbance of trade ties for nonparticipating countries) and possible failure to exploit technological and other advances made elsewhere—may have continued to affect growth even in the 1950's; and thus contributed to the high

---

[3] The algebraic summary is as follows: $r_c^1/r_0 = (b - a)/(1 - a)$, where r_c and r_c^1 are the rates of growth of per capita product in the initial and next period; $b = r_t^1/r_t$, where the r_t's are the rates of growth of total product for the initial and next period; $a = r_p/r_t$, where r_p is the rate of growth of population, the same in both periods. This equation illustrates the relation between the proportional change in the rate of growth of per capita product and b, that in the growth rate of total product. It can be expanded to allow for changes in the rate of growth of population, which need not be assumed constant. The effects would be similar as long as the proportional changes in the growth rate of population are smaller than those in the growth rate of total product.

rates in several of the developed countries of Europe and in Japan. More specifically, the argument is that, even if the material losses of the war had already been made up and per capita product was back to the prewar levels, the accumulated stock of innovations in other countries was available for exploitation; and these additional growth possibilities, reflected in the wider differentials between the per capita products of the European countries and Japan, on the one hand, and those of the United States or Canada, on the other, wider in the late 1940's than in the late 1930's—constituted an important stimulus to continuing high rates of growth—beyond the immediate recovery period and into the 1950's.

The validity of this hypothesis and the extent to which it accounts for the high growth rates in the 1950's shown for several countries in Table 7 can be ascertained only by further analysis. In particular, the specific ways in which the greater backlog of unused innovations has been tapped, and the conditions that had to be met to generate a higher rate of growth, would have to be distinguished and studied. Clearly, it is a crude and incomplete hypothesis, and there may be others—some, in fact, suggested toward the end of the preceding lecture. It may well be that the changes in technology, in institutions, and in attitudes induced by the war had lasting effects—providing conditions favorable to a higher rate of economic growth, even after the end of the postwar recovery period, than prevailed in the long periods before the war. This alternative explanation does not contradict the one suggested above; in a sense it merely shifts the emphasis from the "catching up" process to the exploitation of war-induced technological changes and of the generally large stock of potential innovations, an exploitation more effective because of changes in institutions and attitudes. The reference is to the changed role of government, the greater consensus of society in accepting active responsibility for economic growth, in a readiness to weigh critically, and even discard, long-established notions that may have retarded economic growth in the past. But the hypothesis is not contradictory to that of "catching up" or "making up," for the latter process may also have been accelerated by war-induced changes in institutions and attitudes.

Other hypotheses may reasonably be entertained. Thus, it may be argued that the scientific base of technological innovations underlying modern economic growth has provided an *accelerated* potential, making possible the increasing rates of growth of product per capita despite the decline in input of man-hours per capita. The implication of this hypothesis is that, all other conditions being equal, one should expect an acceleration in the rate of growth even of product per capita; that consequently it is not the higher rate of growth in the 1950's but the significantly lower rate of growth in many countries from 1890 to 1927 than from 1880 to 1913 that needs to be explained. Hence, the explanation for the 1950's lies in the ways and means by which factors that constituted obstacles to potential growth before World War II were removed. Insofar as these ways and means are associated with the war, hot or cold, that induced changes in institutions and attitudes, this hypothesis overlaps the one suggested in the preceding paragraph. But here again the emphasis is shifted: instead of stressing war-induced technological innovations, it stresses the long-term course of technical progress in its impact on potential and actual rates of economic growth.

Finally, long-term swings are evident in the rates of growth of product, total and per capita, and of many components in the product, in a number of developed countries. Such fluctuations, ranging in duration from less than twenty to about forty years, can be observed in the records, and are hardly surprising, since a completely smooth trend line in a relatively rapidly growing economy cannot be expected. These long swings have attracted the attention of scholars, particularly in recent years in connection with the growth experience in the United States.[4] If such long swings do occur, a decade of high growth rates must be compared with earlier periods of relatively high growth rates. A comparison of this sort would indicate whether the magnitudes of the recent decade are distinctive, and whether the factors behind them are different from those in the past. Obviously, this hypothesis of long swings is compatible with the others in the sense that the war, its aftermath, and the subsequent recovery, or catching up, may be viewed as a set of phases in a specific long swing.

Finally, while we have been discussing the European countries and Japan as a group, different causes, and hence different meanings, may be assigned to the high rates of growth in the 1950's in the different countries in the group. Thus, the changes in Japan and Italy may represent a new phase of economic growth, with lastingly higher rates in the future, while the same may not be true of some of the other countries in the group.

(b) Much of the discussion of the high growth rates in the

---

[4] For a preliminary summary of such swings in several countries, see Simon Kuznets, "Quantitative Aspects of the Economic Growth of Nations. I: Levels and Variability of Rates of Growth," *Economic Development and Cultural Change*, 5:44-51 (October 1956). For a convenient summary of the evidence on the United States, see Moses Abramovitz, Statement in the United States 86th Congress, 1st Session, Joint Economic Committee, *Employment, Growth and Price Levels, Hearings*, pt. II (Washington, D.C., 1959), pp. 411-66, and "The Nature and Significance of Kuznets Cycles," *Economic Development and Cultural Change*, 9:225-48 (April 1961). For the United States, see also Simon Kuznets, "Long Swings in the Growth of Population and in Related Economic Variables," *Proceedings of the American Philosophical Society*, 102:25-37 (February 1958), and *Capital in the American Economy*, chaps. 7 and 8; and Bert G. Hickman, "The Postwar Retardation: Another Long Swing in the Rate of Growth," *Papers and Proceedings*, American Economic Association, Spring 1963, which includes an extensive bibliography.

1950's in many developed countries in Europe and in Japan applies also to the relatively low rates of growth in the United States and Canada. The few comments below relate to the United States, the data for which are more familiar to me.

The sensitivity of the rates of growth in per capita income to minor changes in the growth rate of total product can readily be demonstrated for the United States, a country distinguished by a high rate of population growth and a high ratio of population growth to growth of total product (as in Canada). In a paper I prepared two years ago, which provides a convenient record of long-term growth of product, population, and labor force in the United States, summarized in Table 9, the rate of growth in total product (GNP) for the decade from 1948-52 to 1959-61 was 37.6 percent, about a tenth over the rate of 34.1 percent shown in Table 7, line 13, for the decade from 1950-52 to 1960-62. With the rate of growth of population the same, 18.5 percent, that in per capita product is 16.1 percent in the earlier calculation (Table 9, line 8) and 13.2 in Table 7, a difference of two-tenths. Thus a minor shift of a year in dating and the use of somewhat different periods for averaging the terminal values are productive of a perceptible change in the rate of growth of per capita product.

Assuming that the decade rate of growth in per capita product for the 1950's is about 13 percent, several comments are appropriate. First, while this rate is below the long-term average for the United States, it has not been uncommon. Thus in Table 9 we find two other decades with even lower rates—1910-20, and, of course, the depression span from 1929 to 1940; and the rate for 1880-90 is not significantly above 13 percent (and is indeed lower than the 1950-60 rate shown in line 8 of Table 9). A more detailed analysis based on continuous five-year averages would show that these three other periods of relatively low rates of growth in per capita product within the total span since 1880 were the down-phases of long swings.[5]

Second, like the other periods of low growth rates, that for the 1950's followed a period of much higher rates. From Tables 7 and 8 we can calculate that the growth rate in per capita product for the United States must have been 41.2 percent per decade between 1939 and 1951 (the three-year average centered on the latter year)—a rate far higher than any observed for that period in the European countries or in Japan, which show such high rates for the 1950's.

Third, while the rate of growth in the 1950's of product *per capita* was low, compared with the long-term average, the growth in product *per worker* was relatively high (Table 9, columns 4 and 5). The decade of the 1950's was characterized in the United States by a population growth rate that was fairly high compared with the rates since the 1920's; but by a rather low rate of growth in the labor force, reflecting the low birth rates of the depressed 1930's. These long swings, with disparate timing, in the growth rates of population and labor force are of obvious bearing on the interpretation of decadal or similarly short-term rates of growth in per capita and per worker product.

Finally, lines 9-18 of Table 9 illustrate the possible pitfalls in deriving long-term trends even from records for as long a period as the eight decades from 1880 to 1960—given the impact of long swings. The two-decade averages in lines 9-12 suggest no long-term downward trend in the growth rate of per capita product; the three-decade averages in lines 13-15 suggest such a downward trend; and the overlapping four-decade averages in lines 16-18 again deny its existence. Of course, less variable results, even for per capita product, could be obtained by a more systematic scrutiny of the long-term

---

[5] The detailed series are readily available in Kuznets, *Capital in the American Economy*, Table R-26, pp. 563ff.

record than is provided in Table 9; but the point still remains that without such a record and such scrutiny, growth rates over a period as short as a decade may be extremely fallible measures of the rate of long-term growth.

This does not mean, of course, that we need not concern ourselves with these short-term rates of change. Despite the similarity of the low rates of growth of per capita product in the 1950's in the United States to some found in the past, in the down-phases of the long swings; and despite their sequential position, like the earlier ones, after much higher growth rates—much higher than those for the European countries and Japan—these low rates remain an analytical problem, and a matter for concern in connection with policies aimed toward raising them. It may well be that the low growth rate of the 1950's has major distinctive features that make it truly unique; and past experience is no assurance of an automatic adjustment mechanism which can relieve government and society of special concern. For the low-rate periods in the past may have been terminated by some major institutional and policy adjustments, or by some happy historical accident that need not recur again. Nevertheless, the similar periods of the past are an important datum in the formulation of explanations and policies bearing upon the low rates of growth in the 1950's. The existence of precedents focuses attention on specific directions of research and policy considerations that may be far more fruitful than hasty *ad hoc* hypotheses based on the notion that we are facing something entirely new.

(c) In the case of the Communist countries we do encounter something new, and it is the distinctiveness and recent emergence of the Communist organization of economic society that are the sources of the difficulties in evaluating their growth, past or recent. Of course, the primary obstacle is the lack of reliable data, particularly for Mainland China where the statistical blackout has prevented any tested estimates for the years since 1957; and the collapse of the statistical system, so illuminatingly described by Professor Li, makes us wonder whether the Communist government itself possesses adequately comprehensive and reliable data on its country's output.[6] The continuing difficulties that even the older Communist regime in the U.S.S.R. has been having to assure reliable reporting from the field suggests that there is an innate tendency in the organization of the economy to generate inaccurate reporting—with an upward bias resulting from the net advantages of exaggeration to those reporting.

But aside from these problems we face two major difficulties in evaluating economic growth in the Communist countries that stem from our limited experience with economic performance under these regimes. For example, in the case of the U.S.S.R., the Communist regime has operated for over four decades, the supply of data is more plentiful than in any other Communist country (particularly China), and Western scholars have produced valuable tested and carefully revised measures and empirical studies; and yet the stock of accumulated knowledge is inadequate for a thorough evaluation of patterns of change over time. This is hardly surprising since in the three and a half decades that have elapsed since the beginning of the First Five Year Plan in 1928, a full decade was absorbed by the war and the immediate postwar recovery, and important aspects of the regime have changed significantly between the decade and a half (non-war) of Stalin and the decade of Khrushchev. The very growth that took place presented new problems in the 1950's and early 1960's for which there is little precedent in the short history of the Soviet Union.

To illustrate this difficulty we refer to more recent data for

---

[6] See Choh Ming Li, *The Statistical System of Communist China,* University of California Press, Berkeley, 1962.

the U.S.S.R. than those included in the average for 1950-60 in Table 7. According to estimates by Western scholars, the rate of growth of GNP per capita between 1950 and 1958 was 5.0 percent per year, or 63.0 percent per decade—a figure close to that cited in Table 7 (line 18c).[7] But the rate of growth declined to 2.8 percent per year, or 31.8 percent per decade for 1958-62—still substantial but only about half of the earlier level. Since this decline in the growth rate reflects difficulties with agricultural production, which barely rose from the 1958 level, and a perceptible retardation in the rates of growth of industry and construction, one wonders what the response of the Soviet economy will be. The decline in agricultural output during the collectivization years between 1929 and 1933 and the drastic reduction of all output by the end of the war do not seem to be relevant precedents for the recent reduction in the growth rates. Were the high rates in the early 1950's still much affected by the recovery from the war, and is the U.S.S.R. facing a situation that, in the solution of its agricultural problem and in the general adjustment to the completion of any initial phase of rapid economic growth, would mean a new level of growth rates? The question is clearly important, and a detailed sectoral analysis of the economy would be even more helpful than in the case of the developed non-Communist countries whose patterns are more familiar. But even so, the limited historical experience with the Communist regime in the U.S.S.R. bars the promise of easy and firm answers.

The second difficulty is somewhat different, and perhaps more fundamental, in character. In connection with economic growth, we implicitly assume a meaningful relation between the result of economic growth as measured by the product

---

[7] The figures in this paragraph are from "Annual Economic Indicators for the U.S.S.R.," *Joint Economic Committee Print*, 88th Congress, 2nd Session (Washington, D. C., 1964), Table VIII-2, p. 95.

and the desirable goals of economic activity; as well as some minimum requirements as to the mechanism by which growth is attained, in terms of human costs. For obvious reasons we do not compare the economic growth of an ancient country having a large proportion of its output in pyramids produced by slave labor with a modern democratically organized economy that produces a wide variety of consumer goods and relevant capital goods; or, if we do draw such a comparison, we do not accept pyramids at their face value, and severely qualify the comparison in terms of the differences in institutional structure and what it means to desirable human goals other than material goods. The wastes (pyramids) and human costs in the product by which we measure economic growth are large in any society, non-Communist or Communist. But the nature and magnitude of these wastes and costs are genuinely different for non-Communist and Communist societies; and the essential comparability of the two is questionable, even after the Western revision of Communist estimates. Probably the proper recasting of Communist measures of economic growth, which would go much further than that of the measures for the non-Communist societies, would yield different levels of product and different movements over time. We are thus left with the uncomfortable feeling that at present we are comparing incomparables. Greater attention to the consumer goods and related capital investment components of product might help; but even then institutional mechanisms in the two sets of countries would have to be examined carefully, and their meaning, in terms of some specified desirable relations between individuals and society, determined. Although this approach may seem at first to be a futile exercise in applying vague ideals to hard realities, it may prove to be far more—if the desirable relations specified represent a consensus widely shared in the world, as well as conditions indispensable for the efficient operation of economic society at *higher* levels of performance where, unlike the periods of heroic emergencies, individual freedom and consumer sovereignty may be the *sine qua non* for the proper functioning of a developed economy.

(d) The rates of growth in per capita product for the less developed countries of Latin America in the 1950's were somewhat lower than during the preceding decade to decade and a half; whereas the opposite was true of the underdeveloped countries of Asia, where fairly high growth rates in the 1950's were partly making up for lack of growth during the period since the late 1930's. But for present purposes it may be best to concentrate on the findings for the longer period back to the late 1930's, since the cumulative impact of growth for that period may be more significant; and certainly more clearly observable, in comparison with growth in the developed countries.

When so viewed, the findings suggest two observations. First, in Latin America, the rate of growth over the period from 1937 or, still better, from 1927, over 18 percent per decade in per capita product, was about the same as the average growth rate for the non-Communist developed countries. Furthermore, since rates of population growth in Latin America were appreciably higher, the rate of growth of total product was decidedly higher.

Except for the countries that fell below the level of the group as a whole (Argentina, Honduras, Chile), the record of growth in Latin America, both since 1927 and since 1937, may seem satisfactory; and the retardation in the 1950's may seem, like that in the United States and Canada (although it was not so sharp in most Latin American countries), a natural consequence of transient advantages during the war and the immediate postwar years. But setting aside any problems that a more detailed sectoral and component analysis and examination of individual countries may reveal, one relevant question may be raised. With the rate of growth of per capita product since 1927 about the same in Latin America as in the non-Communist developed countries, there could not have been any significant "closing of the gap." The gap remained wide despite the fact that, unlike the European countries and Japan, Latin America suffered no devastation from the war; and despite the presumption that the Latin American countries, as latecomers in the sequence of countries to enter modern economic growth, might have been expected to show higher growth rates than the older developed countries. And yet among the five larger countries distinguished in Table 8, the two with the highest growth in per capita product, Mexico and Colombia, showed rates (somewhat over 20 percent per decade) that were at about the middle of the array for the older developed countries for the same period. Is the failure to realize growth rates in per capita product consistently and significantly higher than 20 percent per decade due to a high rate of population growth; or to problems of size, since many Latin American countries are quite small; or to distinctive social and economic structures which, with their wide inequalities, limit economic growth and make for unstable political structure? And, finally, are the failures, the countries falling behind, due to some temporary aggravation of these social and political difficulties, which are likely to move with time from country to country?

The second broad comment refers to the populous countries of Asia. High as the rate of growth may have been in some of these countries in the 1950's, for most of them the record for the longer period back to the late 1930's reveals quite low rates of growth in per capita product. The gap between per capita product of these countries and those of the older developed countries not only failed to narrow over the period, but must have widened substantially—despite the modest rise in absolute per capita product in most of these less developed countries of Asia. And, if for the sake of total coverage, one raises a question about the less developed countries of Africa, it seems reasonable to guess that by the early 1960's, the rise in their per capita product from the late 1930's could not have begun to approach that of the older developed countries so that here also the gap probably widened.

Thus, for the major regions of less developed countries of the world, the gap between Latin America and the older developed countries was, at best, unchanged; and the gap between Asia and Africa and the developed countries must have grown (and it is likely that the gap vis-à-vis the Communist countries of Europe, but not of Asia, also widened). This maintenance, or further widening, of the gap in per capita product, that is, in relative levels of economic performance, between the older developed countries and the underdeveloped world, was accompanied by far more rapid population growth in the underdeveloped part of the world than in the developed countries. As already noted in the preceding lecture, the rate of growth of population between 1940 and 1960 for the developed part of the world (North and Central Europe, U.S.S.R., North America, and Oceania), a total that ranged from 600 to over 700 million, was 8.5 percent per decade (rising from 3.0 percent for the war decade of 1940-50 to 14.2 percent in 1950-60); whereas that for the underdeveloped part of the world (Asia, Africa, and Latin America, dominated by the huge totals for Asia), ranging from 1.5 to over 2.1 *billion*, was 18.7 percent per decade (and rose from 15.5 percent for 1940-50 to 22.0 percent for 1950-60). In fact, the rates of growth of population and the level of development measured by per capita product were inversely correlated—a correlation not observed in the nineteenth and early decades of the twentieth century. The widening of the gap in per capita product between the developed countries and the large populations of the underdeveloped countries of Asia and possibly of Africa was not necessarily caused by the more rapid rates of population growth in the latter in the recent two decades. But such greater population growth adds to the significance of the widening gap: it increases the weight of the underdeveloped countries in the world population total, and may well constitute a serious obstacle to an orderly and peaceful solution of the pressing problems of economic growth in these areas.

3

The brief account above of postwar economic growth brings our discussion full circle, back to the postwar economic structure of the world reviewed in the first lecture. The diversity among nations, with respect to size, economic development, and political organization, may now be seen as the result of a long history of relatively isolated existence of societies, combined with the recent and uneven spread of economic modernization. The widening of such diversity was associated partly with the capacity of economic societies, once developed, to grow at unusually high rates (despite wars, so far), leaving the others far behind; and partly with increasing nationalism and pressure for political independence, which resulted in the multiplication of sovereign nation-states. The effects of the last war and of the postwar growth differentials, which widened such diversity among nations, have been touched upon. During the course of modern economic growth the interdependence of nations also increased, partly because of technological changes in accessibility through modern channels of transport and communication; and partly because the impressive attainments of economic modernization in developed countries set up ties of dependence and competition, of attraction and repulsion, of cooperation and latent conflict, which, in their universal reach and general intensity, are probably unmatched in the historical past. And here again the effects of the war and of the postwar developments were marked.

Two broad questions are suggested by the observations scattered throughout the lectures; and it may be useful to state them explicitly by way of a postscript.

The first is suggested by the increasing variety of social

and political institutions within which modern economic growth is accommodated—if by economic growth we mean simply a significant sustained rise in aggregate and per capita product and the major accompanying structural changes (shift from agriculture to industry, increase in size of productive unit, greater use of modern technology, and so on). We refer here not only to the authoritarian institutions under which economic growth takes place in Communist countries, but also to the institutional and political differences among the non-Communist developed countries. Thus, emergence of the violent Nazi regime in one of the most economically developed countries of the world raises grave questions about the institutional basis of modern economic growth—if it is susceptible to such a barbaric deformation as a result of transient difficulties.

In short, the problem of the "how" of economic growth, of the ways by which increased product and the related structural changes are achieved—in terms of basic values of human freedom, equality of opportunity, respect for human life, and cooperation with, rather than hostility to, the rest of mankind—is crucial. As measured by the simple criteria of economic output and its structure, modern economic growth has been impressive, and indeed has made revolutionary contributions to the health and material welfare of much of mankind; but its quality in terms of some other human values has been far from high. One could, of course, consider including such values explicitly in the definition and measurement of economic growth; and thus scale down the latter by subtracting noneconomic costs. Yet the difficulties of establishing criteria for measuring these human costs, of devising quantitative tests based on these criteria that would transcend and yet include the purely economic, are obvious—even if in extreme cases they can be seen clearly, as, for example, in the numbers of victims of concentration camps and of political purges, or in the unemployment and poverty of some groups within the developed societies. One should note in this connection that the customary economic measures, which allow primarily for economic costs, perhaps reflect other human costs to a greater degree in the free market-oriented societies than in the authoritarian systems in which concentration of power over human beings is much more extreme.

The point is that in considering the usual measures of economic growth we are in danger of forgetting that one and the same economic result may involve vastly different human costs. And, looking toward the future, one may well ask what other varieties of institutional and political organization, with what other impacts on human values and costs, may emerge to provide auspices for economic growth. Whatever the answer to this question, there is a clear need to supplement the customary measures and analysis of economic growth with more explicit consideration of the kinds of political and institutional framework within which it is to be fitted.

Second, the most disquieting aspect of the changing social framework, within which modern economic growth has been taking place, is the intensified nationalism and its effects on increasingly strained international relations. While it may be semantic license to designate the long period from the end of the Napoleonic wars to World War I as a century of peace, the two sanguinary world wars that marked the last half century do stamp the twentieth century as a distinctive period; and one need hardly emphasize that the emergence, despite greater accessibility, of more sharply divisive boundaries suggested by such a term as the Iron (or Bamboo) Curtain, is a disturbing corollary of the higher rates of economic growth of the recent decades. The increasing strains between the U.S.S.R. and Communist China, so much in the news, are another striking illustration of the great force of divisive nationalism between countries which presumably share a common ideology vis-à-vis the rest of the world. Even in the underdeveloped countries, the intensity of nationalist feelings is productive of continuous international strains and crises, as, for instance, that between India and Pakistan over Kashmir; in the Middle East among the Arab nations, and between them and Israel; in Southeast Asia, between Indonesia and Malaya. And we have no basis for assuming that such strains will diminish or disappear, once vigorous economic growth is attained in these underdeveloped areas. Against such evidence of increasing nationalism one could set the tendencies represented by the Common Market in Europe and similar attempts elsewhere, and by several recent examples of political unions in Asia and Africa. But the balance still seems to be clearly in the direction of intensified and divisive nationalism.

It is easy to argue that with increasing interdependence, the nation-state organization, with the internationally disruptive attitudes and dangerous consequences that it engenders and encourages, has outlived its usefulness; and that the broader aims of mankind would be better served under some kind of unified world political order. But the fact is that the nation-state organization has been continuously, and increasingly, a vehicle for securing consensus and order in the numerous societies into which the world has been divided, to furnish the base for growth under internally acceptable conditions and institutions. It is also easy to argue, as I did toward the end of the second lecture, that a national consensus need not be based on hostility to others, often consciously promoted in order to intensify a nation's unity and preparedness for the drastic measures that are considered essential for accelerating economic growth. But the fact is that recourse to such divisive ways of promoting national unity has been increasing, not decreasing, in many countries. And it is difficult to dismiss the association between intensification of divisive nationalism, combined increasingly with the authoritarian cast of the political system, and the spread of modern economic growth across the face of the globe—on the assumption that such an association lacks elements of indispensability, not only in logic but even within the long-term context of modern world history.

Looking into the future, one may well ask whether there is much basis for assuming that these trends will not continue; and if they do continue, whether it will be possible to contain their consequences and prevent another worldwide war— with destructive effects on the material and spiritual welfare of mankind that may far transcend, both in absolute and proportional magnitudes, anything experienced so far. One could derive some comfort from the hypothesis that aggressive nationalism may be most virulent when a nation is in the early phases of its modern economic growth and still too weak to do much harm; and is likely to abate as greater economic and social maturity is reached and the resulting rise in living standards may create groups with sufficient power to confine (within tolerable limits) aggressive policies toward the rest of the world. After all, there seems to have been such a trend in the brief but violent history of the U.S.S.R. But this hypothesis may assign too much weight to economic interests and too little to the political forces and the internal logic of dictatorships, and, moreover, still leaves much room for dangerous tensions and for the question whether such social maturity is reached before or after a punishing war.

The two broad questions raised above concerning the institutional framework of modern economic growth, in its bearing, first, on human values and costs to the country's population, and, second, on the possible consequences to the rest of the world and world peace, are of major relevance in considering the future of any group of countries, developed or underdeveloped, libertarian or authoritarian. The specific aspect of social organization and the specific problem stressed in these questions will differ from one to another. Thus for an advanced democratic society like that of the United States, the major aspect likely to be emphasized is the relation between the apparent sources of future economic growth, lying in some complexes of technological innovations and consumer demand, on the one hand, and requirements for employment and the distribution of employment opportunities, on the other—a problem that may underlie current preoccupation with chronically backward areas and chronically underemployed and economically deprived minorities. And the manner in which this problem is resolved would clearly bear also on the contribution that the U. S. economy can make to economic growth elsewhere. The specific aspects that the questions of the interplay between institutional conditions and economic growth may assume in a country like the U.S.S.R. would be quite different. They might lie in the conflicts between the rigidities of the political organization of a single party system and authoritarian government, the requirements of greater efficiency in many sectors of the productive system, the emergence of groups that demand more freedom in choosing a pattern of life, and the challenge to the leadership of the U.S.S.R. Communist party abroad. And with respect to the wide variety of underdeveloped countries, important as the question is whether these countries will succeed at all in tapping the wide potential of modern economic growth, an even more important question is *how* they will do it, in terms of costs to themselves and to others.

It is hardly necessary, nor am I competent, to illustrate further the variety of specific aspects which the general questions on the relation between institutional framework and economic growth assume, in application either to past or future economic growth in various parts of the world. But by way of further observation drawing upon earlier discussion, I shall comment on a specific implication of the questions as they relate to the proximate future of underdeveloped countries. For it is in this area that the implication of these questions concerning the connection between institutional and political change and economic growth stand out most clearly.

Tables 1 and 2 show that of the total population of under-developed countries, defined as those with per capita gross product of less than $200 in 1958, that is, of some 1.7 billion out of a world total in 1958 of 2.9 billion, well over 1.4 billion are in Asia, and half of the latter is accounted for by Mainland China and its satellites. Obviously, developments in Mainland China will put their stamp on the proximate future of the large masses of low-income populations in Asia; for a rise in the per capita product of the former to the rather modest level of $200 would make its total magnitude—and thus possibly the surplus divertible for exercise of power abroad—not much smaller than that of the U.S.S.R. today, and surely among the larger divertible surpluses on the Eurasian continent. The effects are already apparent in the looming role that the growing economic and political bulk of Mainland China is assuming in the development of its neighbors to the south—in particular of the former states of Indo-China and further toward Indonesia, but also among the countries on the Indian subcontinent. The resolution of many problems of effective institutional organization for the accommodation of economic growth will occur, in Asia and perhaps elsewhere, within a political context in which developments in Mainland China, both domestic and in foreign relations, will play a significant part. For some of its smaller neighbors this may mean a forced adoption of Communist regimes. For India and other larger neighbors it will mean a challenge that may test national unity and perhaps accelerate the modernization of the political fabric. And it may well have wide ramification elsewhere, as has repeatedly been the case in the historical past when some one large national unit entered a period of economic modernization, with spreading effects on its neighbors and on international relations over much of the world.

The hard core of these speculations is the judgment that the political and institutional factors may be more important than the purely economic (such as relative supplies of labor, capital, and so forth) particularly when they relate to a large nation. The same judgment as to the importance of political and institutional factors in the economic future of underdeveloped areas would also be true of much of Africa and Latin America, with the significant difference that these continents are not likely to be as directly affected by a single emergent giant nation in the early and aggressive phases of its economic growth. Nor is this judgment, which implies limits to the contributions of purely economic analysis to growth problems of underdeveloped countries, surprising. The trends in the recent study of economic growth have pointed up the importance of social and political institutions as distinct from traditional economic variables. The findings, referred to in the second lecture, which repeatedly showed the small proportional contribution made to growth of product per capita by the increase in simple inputs per capita, while naturally stressing the importance of "technological progress" also imply that large weights should be attached to the institutional and social arrangements that govern the methods by which knowledge and the purely economic factors are used. The variability, in both time and space, of the coefficients in the economic production functions, points in the same direction. And the recently increased emphasis on education and other investment in human beings is bound to lead to the recognition that the social and political institutions, not the purely economic, condition the flow of human resources, both in their acquisition of characteristics important in economic performance and in their allocation to various tasks within the economy. If, then, the main question in the economic growth of underdeveloped countries is how to make the institutional changes that would permit effective functioning of the purely economic variables, and do it without great human costs, it is hardly surprising that emphasis is on the political and institutional changes that are likely to emerge as a framework within which greater economic growth will be attained.

It is not our intention to argue that the institutional and political framework must be given; and that the economic processes must wait until such institutional "preconditions" exist. Some of these preconditions are in fact induced by economic growth itself. And yet granted the interplay between the two, even the possibility of substitution among various institutional and political preconditions for economic growth does not diminish their importance, or the importance of their variety as affected by the diverse heritages of the large group of underdeveloped countries today.

These concluding remarks place the contribution of economic measurement and analysis to the understanding of economic growth processes and policies in a limiting perspective. If modern economic growth is, in essence, a controlled revolution in economy and society, and the revolution in society, with its internal and external ramifications, is an indispensable part of the total process, economic growth is neither fully understood, nor properly measurable and analyzable, in a study limited to traditionally defined economic variables. Yet, in our awareness of the limits of our knowledge, we still cannot afford to neglect what we do know, and to dismiss as worthless the hard economic facts and the contributions of analysis of purely economic variables. The perspective rather suggests extending both measurement and analysis to cover at least the economic aspects of a wider variety of social and political processes, of a wider range of their differences over time and across space. It is this extension of the range of economic and social growth experience under measurement and analysis that promises to yield additional insights, without a forced neglect of the few empirical findings and analytical relations that have already been established.

TABLE 7. DECADAL RATES OF GROWTH IN THE 1950's AND FROM THE LATE 1930's TO THE EARLY 1960's, TOTAL PRODUCT, POPULATION, AND PER CAPITA PRODUCT (*percentages*)

	The 1950's				Late 1930's to Early 1960's			
	Period (1)	Product (2)	Popu- lation (3)	Per capita product (4)	Period (5)	Product (6)	Popu- lation (7)	Per capita product (8)
I. NON-COMMUNIST DEVELOPED COUNTRIES								
1. Belgium	1950-52 to 1960-62	34.3	5.8	26.9	1938 to 1960-62	24.5	4.1	19.6
2. Denmark	1950-52 to 1960-62	45.8	7.3	35.9	1939 to 1960-62	32.6	9.2	21.4
3. Finland	1950-52 to 1960-62	58.9	10.4	43.9	1938 to 1960-62	36.6	9.1	25.2
4. France	1950-52 to 1960-62	55.1	9.3	41.9	1937 to 1960-62	27.2	4.7	21.5
5. Netherlands	1950-52 to 1960-62	60.2	13.4	41.3	1937 to 1960-62	37.0	13.5	20.7
6. Norway	1950-52 to 1960-62	43.2	9.6	30.7	1939 to 1960-62	35.5	9.6	23.6
7. United Kingdom	1950-52 to 1960-62	30.2	4.7	24.4	1937 to 1960-62	17.3	4.8	11.9

TABLE 7. (*Continued*)

	The 1950's				Late 1930's to Early 1960's			
	Period (1)	Product (2)	Population (3)	Per capita product (4)	Period (5)	Product (6)	Population (7)	Per capita product (8)
8. Austria	1950-52 to 1960-62	72.2	2.1	68.7	1938 to 1960-62	31.6	2.1	28.9
9. West Germany	1950-52 to 1960-62	102.6	11.7	81.4	1936 to 1960-62	47.1	14.9	28.0
10. Italy	1950-52 to 1960-62	78.2	5.8	68.4	1939 to 1960-62	38.0	6.4	29.7
11. Sweden	1950-52 to 1960-62	45.9	6.3	37.3	1939 to 1960-62	49.8	8.2	38.4
12. Switzerland	1950-52 to 1957-59	48.2	13.8	30.2	1938 to 1957-59	31.9	11.2	18.6
13. United States	1950-52 to 1960-62	34.1	18.5	13.2	1939 to 1960-62	48.7	16.4	27.7
14. Canada	1950-52 to 1960-62	43.6	30.4	10.1	1939 to 1960-62	58.3	23.1	28.6
15. Australia	1950/51-52/53 to 1959/60-61/62	46.0	24.8	17.0	1938/39 to 1959/60-61/62	44.8	19.9	20.8

TABLE 7. (*Continued*)

	The 1950's				Late 1930's to Early 1960's			
	Period (1)	Product (2)	Popu- lation (3)	Per capita product (4)	Period (5)	Product (6)	Popu- lation (7)	Per capita product (8)
16. New Zealand	1950/51 to 1960/61	45.7	24.5	17.0	1937/38 to 1960/61	35.6	19.1	13.9
17. Japan	1950-52 to 1959-61	143.0	12.2	116.6	1939 to 1959-61	42.9	14.1	25.2
II. COMMUNIST COUNTRIES								
18. U.S.S.R.								
a. Official	1950-52 to 1960-62	150.0	19.0	110.1	1940 to 1960-62	105.9	5.4	95.4
b. Official	1949-51 to 1959-61	172.2	18.9	128.9	1940 to 1959-61	107.9	4.8	98.4
c. Revised	1950 to 1960	93.1	18.9	62.4	1940 to 1960	52.1	4.8	45.1
19. Bulgaria								
a. Official	1950-52 to 1960-62	130.8	9.4	111.0	1939 to 1960-62	73.1	11.2	55.7
b. Revised	1950-52 to 1960-62	70.1	9.4	55.5	1939 to 1960-62	35.9	11.2	22.2

TABLE 7. (*Continued*)

	The 1950's				Late 1930's to Early 1960's			
	Period (1)	Product (2)	Population (3)	Per capita product (4)	Period (5)	Product (6)	Population (7)	Per capita product (8)
20. Czechoslovakia								
a. Official	1950-52 to 1960-62	97.3	10.0	79.4	1938 to 1960-62	51.9	—2.5	55.8
b. Revised	1950-52 to 1960-62	53.7	10.0	39.7	1938 to 1960-62	12.7	—2.5	15.6
21. East Germany, revised	1950 to 1958	87.2	—7.0	101.3	1936 to 1958	9.1	3.3	5.6
22. Hungary								
a. Official	1950-52 to 1960-62	78.6	6.4	67.9	1938 to 1960-62	48.9	4.0	43.2
b. Revised	1950-52 to 1960-62	42.6	6.4	34.0	1938 to 1960-62	18.1	4.0	13.6
23. Poland								
a. Official	1950-52 to 1960-62	111.3	18.6	78.2	1938 to 1960-62	73.3	—3.1	78.8
b. Revised	1950-52 to 1960-62	65.0	18.6	39.1	1938 to 1960-62	11.8	—3.1	15.4

TABLE 7. (*Continued*)

	The 1950's				Late 1930's to Early 1960's			
	Period (1)	Product (2)	Population (3)	Per capita product (4)	Period (5)	Product (6)	Population (7)	Per capita product (8)
24. Rumania								
a. Official	1950-52 to 1960-62	137.5	12.8	110.5	1938 to 1960-62	58.7	7.9	47.1
b. Revised	1950-52 to 1960-62	75.1	12.8	55.2	1938 to 1960-62	30.7	7.9	21.1
25. Yugoslavia								
a. Official	1952-54 to 1960-62	131.3	11.6	107.3	not available			
b. Revised	1952-54 to 1960-62	71.4	11.6	53.6	1938 to 1960-62	30.9	8.6	20.5
26. Mainland China								
a. Official	1952-54 to 1957-59	227.2	23.1	165.8	not available			
b. Revised, 1933 prices	1952-54 to 1955-57	57.6	24.8	26.3	1933 to 1955-57	14.1	9.9	3.8
c. Revised, 1952 prices	1952-54 to 1957-59	115.7	27.9	68.6	1933 to 1957-59	28.7	11.5	15.4

[133]

TABLE 7. (Continued)

	The 1950's				Late 1930's to Early 1960's			
	Period (1)	Product (2)	Population (3)	Per capita product (4)	Period (5)	Product (6)	Population (7)	Per capita product (8)
III. NON-COMMUNIST LESS DEVELOPED COUNTRIES								
27. Greece	1950-52 to 1960-62	84.4	9.9	67.8	1938 to 1960-62	21.9	7.5	13.4
28. Argentina [see note]	1950-52 to 1960-62	15.2	20.0	—4.0	1935-39 to 1960-62	27.9	20.4	6.2
29. Brazil	1950-52 to 1959-61	76.4	36.9	28.9	1935-39 to 1959-61	59.6	30.2	22.6
30. Mexico	1950-52 to 1960-62	76.8	35.7	30.3	1935-39 to 1960-62	79.7	31.4	36.8
31. Chile	1950-52 to 1960-62	37.8	26.6	8.8	1935-39 to 1960-62	41.1	22.2	15.5
32. Colombia	1950-52 to 1959-61	58.1	24.6	26.9	1935-39 to 1959-61	54.6	24.5	24.2
33. Ecuador	1950-52 to 1960-62	58.4	37.0	15.6	1939 to 1960-62	67.7	32.2	26.9
34. Honduras	1950-52 to 1959-61	41.3	34.3	5.2	1938 to 1959-61	47.6	26.4	16.8

TABLE 7. (Continued)

	The 1950's				Late 1930's to Early 1960's			
	Period (1)	Product (2)	Popu- lation (3)	Per capita product (4)	Period (5)	Product (6)	Popu- lation (7)	Per capita product (8)
35. Puerto Rico	1950-52 to 1960-62	92.5	7.8	78.6	1938 to 1960-62	90.0	13.2	67.8
36. Latin America, total	1950-52 to 1954-56	51.4	26.9	19.3	1935-39 to 1954-56	55.2	24.2	25.0
37. Burma	1950-52 to 1960-62	65.9	15.3	43.9	1938 to 1960-62	5.6	14.4	—7.7
38. Cambodia	1951-53 to 1957-59	52.2	30.4	16.7	1938 to 1957-59	34.5	22.8	9.5
39. Ceylon	1950-52 to 1960-62	38.5	29.1	7.3	1938 to 1960-62	65.4	27.4	29.8
40. Taiwan	1950-52 to 1960-62	108.2	42.2	46.4	1938 to 1960-62	44.8	33.2	8.7
41. India	1950/51-1952/53 to 1959/ 60-1961/ 62	42.6	21.4	17.5	1937/38-1939/40 to 1959/ 60-1961/ 62	22.5	16.6	5.1

[135]

TABLE 7. (Continued)

	The 1950's				Late 1930's to Early 1960's			
	Period (1)	Product (2)	Population (3)	Per capita product (4)	Period (5)	Product (6)	Population (7)	Per capita product (8)
42. Indonesia	1951-53 to 1957-59	49.9	23.4	21.5	1938 to 1957-59	13.1	14.3	—1.0
43. Pakistan	1952-54 to 1960-62	30.7	23.4	5.9		not available		
44. Philippines	1950-52 to 1960-62	72.3	37.1	25.7	1938 to 1960-62	35.0	29.7	4.1
45. Turkey	1950-52 to 1960-62	66.7	32.2	26.1	1938 to 1960-62	44.9	25.3	15.6
46. Thailand	1951-53 to 1960-62	67.8	27.8	31.3	1938 to 1960-62	73.1	23.4	40.3

Product figures are in constant prices; and for recent years, unless otherwise indicated, are from the U. N. Statistical Office records.

Population, for the midyear of periods for which averages of product were taken, are from the *Demographic Yearbook, 1960* and *1962*, unless otherwise indicated.

Rates were calculated directly for two of the three series and for the third were derived from the relatives of those two.

Line 1: Carbonnelle, Table 1, p. 358 for total product, 1938 to 1950-52.

Lines 2-14, 21, 27, 30, 36-38, 40-42, 44, 45: Sources cited in the notes to Table 6 for total product.

Line 15: Clark, Table IX, pp. 90-91, for 1938/39 to 1948/49; by letter from B. D. Haig of the Australian National University for 1948/49 to 1953/54 for total product.

Line 16: Clark, Table XXX, pp. 171-72, for 1937/38 to 1951/52 for total product. For later years the rate of growth of per capita product was assumed the same as that for Australia (suggested by a comparison of the current price per capita figures in the *Yearbook of National Accounts Statistics, 1962,* Table 3, p. 317).

Line 17: Rosovsky-Ohkawa unpublished revisions of the Ohkawa tables for total product and population.

Line 18: Official: U. N., *Statistical Papers,* Ser. H, No. 8, for 1940 to 1950 for total product.
Revised: Bergson, *Real National Income,* Table 51, p. 210, for 1940 to 1950; Cohn, Table 3, p. 75, for 1950 to 1960 for total product.
Population: Bergson, *Real National Income,* Table K-1, p. 442, for 1940 to 1950; Brackett, Appendix Table A-1, p. 555, for 1950 to 1960.

Lines 19, 20, 22-25: Official: For lines 19, 22, and 24 the sources cited are those in the notes to Table 6; for lines 20 and 23 U. N., *Statistical Papers,* Ser. H, No. 8; for line 25, U. N. Statistical Office records for total product.
Revised: Based on two assumptions: (a) that the rate of growth of per capita product in the 1950's was about half of the official rate (suggested by the figures for the U.S.S.R.) and (b) that the prewar per capita product was the same as that for the beginning of the 1950's.

Line 26: Official: U. N. Statistical Office records for total product. *Revised:* From the sources cited in the notes to Table 6.

Lines 28, 29, 31, and 32: Ganz, Table II, p. 225, for 1935-39 to 1950-54 for total product. The estimates for Argentina are now under revision, which indicates a distinctly higher rate of growth. The revised series suggest a rate of growth in product per capita in the 1950's of 8 to 10 percent per decade instead of a decline—with corresponding effects on the rates in columns 2, 6, and 8. At the time of going to press the final revised estimates had not been completed and could not be incorporated here.

Line 33: U. N. Statistical Office records for total product.

Lines 34 and 35: U. N., *Satistical Papers,* Ser. H, No. 8, for 1938 to 1950 and 1938/39 to 1948/49, respectively, for total product.

Line 39: Henry M. Oliver, Jr., "The Economy of Ceylon," in Calvin B. Hoover, ed., *Economic Systems of the Commonwealth* (Durham, 1962), Table 5, p. 223, for 1938 to 1950 for per capita product.

Line 43: U. N. Statistical Office records for total product.

Line 46: U. N., *Statistical Papers,* Ser. H, No. 9, for 1938 to 1951 for total product.

TABLE 8. DECADAL RATES OF GROWTH, 1927-60 AND EARLIER LONG PERIODS, PRODUCT, POPULATION, AND PER CAPITA PRODUCT, SELECTED COUNTRIES (*percentages*)

		1890-1927	1880-1913	1880-1960	1960 as Relative of 1880
	1927-60 (1)	(2)	(3)	(4)	(5)
A. DEVELOPED COUNTRIES					
Belgium					
1. Product	15.8	27.2	31.6	22.2	509
2. Population	4.5	7.7	10.8	6.4	165
3. Per capita	10.8	18.1	18.8	14.8	308
Denmark					
4. Product	31.0	33.1	40.5	32.7	992
5. Population	8.7	11.9	11.5	10.3	222
6. Per capita	20.5	18.9	26.0	20.3	447
France					
7. Product	16.4	21.6	26.2	19.5	420
8. Population	3.7	0.5	1.9	2.1	118
9. Per capita	12.2	21.0	23.8	17.0	356
Netherlands					
10. Product	27.1	31.6	20.7	26.2	658
11. Population	13.5	15.3	12.8	13.6	280
12. Per capita	12.0	14.1	7.0	11.1	235
Norway					
13. Product	38.2	27.8	24.2	30.3	865
14. Population	8.1	9.3	7.6	8.1	188
15. Per capita	27.8	16.9	15.4	20.5	460
Germany					
16. Product	39.8	19.6	33.1	29.8	815
17. Population	13.0	10.1	12.7	11.2	236
18. Per capita	23.7	8.6	18.1	16.7	345
Italy					
19. Product	30.6	20.5	17.1	22.6	520
20. Population	7.0	6.6	7.3	6.8	170
21. Per capita	22.1	13.0	9.1	14.8	306

TABLE 8. (*Continued*)

		1927-60 (1)	1890-1927 (2)	1880-1913 (3)	1880-1960 (4)	1960 as Relative of 1880 (5)
	Sweden					
22.	Product	45.9	34.1	36.5	37.5	1,319
23.	Population	6.4	6.7	6.5	6.3	164
24.	Per capita	37.1	25.7	28.2	29.4	804
	Switzerland					
25.	Product	33.9	27.3	26.8	30.3	604
26.	Population	8.7	8.7	13.3	8.7	176
27.	Per capita	23.2	17.1	11.9	19.9	343
	United Kingdom					
28.	Product	19.3	11.9	27.6	18.2	387
29.	Population	4.6	5.3	8.7	5.4	153
30.	Per capita	14.1	6.2	17.4	12.1	253
	United States					
31.	Product	33.1	43.0	46.1	38.9	1,435
32.	Population	13.5	18.5	22.1	17.2	361
33.	Per capita	17.3	20.7	19.7	18.5	398
	Canada					
34.	Product	40.7	37.8	45.2	39.0	1,436
35.	Population	19.7	21.0	19.6	19.3	418
36.	Per capita	17.5	13.9	21.4	16.5	344
	Japan					
37.	Product	42.9	45.6	37.8	42.0	1,658
38.	Population	13.4	12.3	10.9	12.3	253
39.	Per capita	26.0	29.7	24.3	26.4	655

		Argentina (1)	Brazil (2)	Chile (3)	Colombia (4)	Mexico (5)	Latin America (6)
	B. LATIN AMERICA						
40.	Product	24.0[a]	51.7	35.8	52.3	56.4	44.9
41.	Population	21.2	27.8	20.2	23.7	27.6	22.0
42.	Per capita	2.3[a]	18.7	13.0	23.1	22.6	18.8

[a] Under revision; see note to line 28 of Table 7.

NOTES

Product is in constant prices and for recent years beyond those specified below are from the U. N. Statistical Office records. Population is generally for the midyear of a period when product is an average for more than one year, and for years beyond those specified below is from the *Demographic Yearbook, 1960* and *1962*.

Rates for per capita product are derived from relatives for total product and population.

Since continuous series are not available for the entire long period, 1880 to 1962, various series have been linked as indicated in the notes below.

The shorter periods are 1878-82 to 1913, 1888-92 to 1925-29, and 1925-29 to 1960-62, unless otherwise indicated.

Belgium: The shorter periods are 1880 to 1913, 1890 to 1927, 1927 to 1960-62.

Line 1: Clark, Table XI, pp. 101-02, for 1880 and 1890 (interpolated between 1846 and 1895) and for 1913; Carbonnelle, Table 1, p. 170, for 1913, 1927, and 1948.

Line 2: Derived from Clark, Table XI, pp. 101-02, for 1880, 1890, and 1913; from Bunlé, Table 1, p. 170, for 1913 and 1920.

Denmark:

Line 4: Bjerke-Ussing, Table III, pp. 146-47, for 1878-82 to 1950-52.

Line 5: Bjerke-Ussing, Table I, pp. 142-43, for 1880, 1890, 1913; Bunlé, Table 1, p. 171, for 1920 comparable with 1913.

France: The shorter periods are the average of 1871-80 and 1881-90 to 1913, the average of 1881-90 and 1891-1900 to 1925-29, and 1925-29 to 1960-62.

Line 7: Kuznets, "Quantitative Aspects . . . ," Table 3, p. 59, for 1871-80 to 1913; Svennilson, Table A.1, p. 233, for 1913, 1925-29, and 1950.

Line 8: Kuznets, "Quantitative Aspects . . . ," Table 3, p. 59, for 1871-80 to 1913; Svennilson, Table A.4, p. 236, for 1913, 1927, and 1950.

Netherlands: The shorter periods are 1880 to 1913, 1900 to 1925-29, and 1925-29 to 1960-62.

Line 10: Interpolated for 1880 between 1860 and 1900, which were obtained by letter from J. B. D. Derksen; *Nationale Rekeningen, 1954,* Table 18, p. 93, for 1900, 1913, 1925-29, and 1950-52.

Line 11: Interpolated for 1880 between 1860 and 1900, which were obtained by letter from J. B. D. Derksen; Central Bureau of Statistics, *Het Nationale Inkomen van Nederland, 1921-1939* (Utrecht, 1948), Table 45, p. 50, for 1900 and 1927.

Norway: The shorter periods are 1875-84 to 1913, 1885-94 to 1925-29, and 1925-29 to 1960-62.

Line 13: Bjerke, Table IV.3, p. 32, for 1875-84, 1885-95, 1905-14, and 1920-29; *National Accounts, 1900-1929,* Table 14, pp. 128-29, for 1905-14 and 1913, 1920-29 and 1925-29, and 1950.

Line 14: Bjerke, Table II.3, p. 14, for 1880, 1890, and 1900; *National Accounts, 1900-1929,* Table 14, pp. 128-29, for 1900, 1913, and 1927.

Germany: The shorter periods are 1876-85 to 1913, 1886-95 to 1925-29, and 1925-29 to 1960-62.

Line 16: Hoffmann and Müller, Table 2, p. 14 for 1876-85, 1886-95, and Table 14, pp. 39-40 for 1913; Jostock, Table I, p. 82 for 1913, 1925-29, 1935-37, 1936, and 1950-52.

Line 17: Hoffmann and Müller, Table 14, pp. 39-40 for 1880, 1890, and 1913; Jostock, Table I, p. 82 for 1913, 1925-29, 1935-37, 1936, and 1950-52 (derived from total and per capita product).

Italy:

Lines 19 and 20: Indagine . . . , Table 37, pp. 251-52 for 1878-82 to 1950.

Sweden:

Line 22: Johansson, Table 18, pp. 62-65 for 1878-82 to 1950-52.

Line 23: Lindahl, Dahlgren, and Kock, Part II, Table 64, pp. 4-5 for 1880 to 1927.

Switzerland: The shorter periods are 1890 to 1913, 1890 to 1925-29, and 1925-29 to 1957-59.

Line 25: Clark, Table XXXVIII, pp. 187-89 for 1890 to 1951; U. N., *Statistical Papers,* Ser. H, No. 9 for 1951 and 1954.

Line 26: Clark, Table XXXVIII, pp. 187-89 for 1890 to 1927 (derived from total and per capita product).

United Kingdom:

Lines 28 and 29: Deane and Cole, Table 90, pp. 329-31 for 1878 to 1950-52.

United States:

Lines 31 and 32: Kuznets, *Capital in the American Economy,* annual data underlying Table R-26, pp. 563-64 and Table R-37, pp. 624-27 for 1878-82 to 1929-33; *Economic Report of the President, January 1964,* Table C-3, p. 210 and Table C-16, p. 227 for 1929-33 to 1960-62, the latter adjusted to exclude Alaska and Hawaii.

Canada:

Lines 34 and 35: Firestone, Table 87, p. 276 for 1878 to 1950 for product, and Table 83, pp. 240-41 for 1880 to 1927 for population.

Japan: The shorter periods are 1879-81 to 1913, 1888-92 to 1925-29, and 1925-29 to 1959-61.

Lines 37 and 38: Rosovsky-Ohkawa unpublished tables.

Latin America: The period is 1925-29 to 1960-62 for Argentina, Chile, and Mexico; 1925-29 to 1959-61 for Brazil and Colombia; 1925-29 to 1954-56 for Latin America.

Line 40: Ganz, Table II, p. 225, for 1925-29 and 1950-54 for all countries except Mexico; Lopez, Table 2, pp. 587-89, for 1925-29 and 1950-52 for Mexico; Ganz, Table III, p. 226, for 1954-56 for Latin America.

Line 41: Ganz, Table III, p. 226, for 1927 and 1955 for Latin America.

TABLE 9. DECADAL RATES OF GROWTH, GROSS NATIONAL PRODUCT, POPULATION, AND LABOR FORCE, UNITED STATES, 1880-1960 (*percentages*)

		Gross National Product (1)	Population (2)	Labor Force (3)	Product per Capita (4)	Product per Worker (5)
	Decades					
1.	1880-90	44.2	25.0	30.5	15.3	10.5
2.	1890-1900	48.6	19.5	28.0	24.3	16.1
3.	1900-10	44.0	21.3	30.1	18.7	10.6
4.	1910-20	29.3	16.1	11.0	11.4	16.4
5.	1920-29	47.9	15.7	14.3	27.8	29.3
6.	1929-40	14.6	7.7	12.8	6.4	1.6
7.	1940-50	51.9	14.8	14.9	32.3	32.2
8.	1950-60	37.6	18.5	12.6	16.1	22.2
	Longer Periods					
9.	1880-1900	46.4	22.3	29.3	19.7	13.3
10.	1900-20	36.4	18.6	20.2	15.0	13.5
11.	1920-40	28.5	11.2	13.5	15.6	13.2
12.	1940-60	44.6	16.6	13.7	23.9	27.1
13.	1880-1910	45.6	21.9	29.6	19.4	12.4
14.	1900-29	39.9	17.7	18.4	18.8	18.2
15.	1929-60	33.1	13.4	13.4	17.4	17.4
16.	1880-1920	41.3	20.4	24.6	17.3	13.4
17.	1900-40	32.4	14.9	16.8	15.3	13.4
18.	1920-60	36.3	13.9	13.6	19.7	20.0

NOTES

For the underlying series and sources see Simon Kuznets, "Notes on the Pattern of U. S. Economic Growth," in Edgar O. Edwards, ed., *The Nation's Economic Objectives*, Rice University Semicentennial Series (University of Chicago, 1964) Table 1, p. 16.

The rates of growth were calculated for gross national product (constant prices), population, and labor force from five-year averages centered on the terminal year of the decade as shown in the stub—except for 1940 and 1960, for which three-year averages were used, and 1929 for which the single value was used.

Entries in lines 9-18 are geometric means of the decadal rates in lines 1-8, with due allowance for the slight differences in duration of the periods in lines 5 and 6.

INDEX

The letter "t" following a page number indicates reference is to table.